J. Daniel Mathein • Morris B. Squire

How To Make Decisions That Pay Off

- THE EFFECTIVE
- MANAGER'S GUIDE
- TO CREATIVE
- PROBLEM SOLVING

pluribus press

DIVISION OF TEACH 'EM INC

CHICAGO 1982

89   88   87   86   85   5   4   3

Library of Congress Catalog Card Number:
81-85832

International Standard Book Number:
0-931028-27-2 (Paperbound)
0-931028-28-0 (Clothbound)

Pluribus Press, Division of Teach 'em, Inc.
160 East Illinois Street
Chicago, Illinois 60611

Printed in the United States of America

To the people of the world —
one better decision
one step forward

TABLE OF CONTENTS

chapter one
INTRODUCTION

This examination of the process of creatively generating ideas and evaluating those ideas is an outgrowth of years of effort in the area of health and productivity improvement.

In the summer of 1974 Morris B. Squire, President of Forest Hospital and Foundation, initiated a program for the employees of Forest Hospital designed to assist in health improvement. Employees were instructed to write personal goals in the areas of Nutrition, Exercise, and Stress Management in addition to the classic Management By Objective (MBO) area of work goals.

From 1974 to 1978 the program was expanded to include Social/Emotional and Leisure Goals while the Work area was changed to Work/Education. As a six parameter personal growth program, it generated positive results in the areas of improved health and productivity, as evidenced by a reduction of sick days taken by employees.

During the fall of 1978 the final, and, perhaps, key ingredient was added to what is now called the Personal Management System. That key ingredient—the power behind all human endeavor—is creativity.

We encourage all employees to expand their ability to create—in all areas of their lives. We very quickly found that to encourage individuals to create—and to actually see creative results—were often miles apart.

Reviewing the situation brought to light the problem of making decisions. It appeared relatively easy to generate ideas. Perhaps too easy! So many ideas or life options were created that individuals often had difficulty making decisions as to which was the proper course of action to follow. Much time and energy went into non-productive, low-payback areas. To solve this problem we needed a program to teach our employees problem-solving techniques. Most processes available at that time were designed solely for large organizations, utilizing large inputs of time, energy and resources. We wanted a program incorporating flexibility, speed, reliability and minimal expense.

Several consultants were retained; many processes were evaluated; and much time was invested in the recombination of existing processes into the program we currently teach employees. The instruction of a group takes less than one hour and has proven most beneficial in cementing together all seven areas of Personal Management System.

Having successfully used this process for three years, we wish to share our experiences so that others may benefit through the use of this flexible decision-making model.

To place realistic boundaries to this endeavor this book will explain the mechanics and application of a decision-making method which does not require an undue input of time, manpower or resources. Realizing that most decisions are based upon the past (i.e., what worked before and back to the basics), we encourage you, while reading, to release your learned restraints—expand your potential options and make your decisions without using the words *should* or *can't.*

This study of *creative decision-making* will combine mind expanding and "brainstorm" techniques. Upon the ideas generated from these efforts we will overlay an evaluation method which is simple and universally applicable. The idea generation produces options—the evaluation procedure identifies the areas of high payback thus simplifying the decision-making process.

Fast track format

The format of this book might be considered creative in itself. The book is written in what the authors call "fast track." In many books it is necessary for the casual reader to wade through reams of seemingly useless technical, research, or background data to find the keys to a process. Not here. In this volume the backbone data well be presented at the beginning of each chapter in larger type. In the body (smaller type) of each chapter you will find examples and supplemental data. Should you question the validity of any point—good—because your questioning mind can add to the base of knowledge comprising human experience.

Accompanying this book you will find a study guide with all the forms and related material you will need. If someone else has used the study guide—no matter, you can do all of the exercises without the study guide. All you'll need is a few sheets of paper.

Plunge in, the water is fine

To get the benefits you should from this book, you will have to participate. Please do. None of the exercises we ask you to perform are difficult. But they are important. The lessons you will learn about yourself and your approach to creativity will serve you well the rest of your life—when the rest of this book may be only a distant memory. So, please, do yourself a favor and complete the assignments that are an essential part of reading this book. You will be glad you did. We promise you.

chapter two
HOW WE THINK

Each of us has the ability to create. To explain this power we would like you to take a base line measurement (the only way to measure growth is to know where you started). Below is a simple experiment.

Practice #1 instructions

The situation is this: I need your help. I am the president of a firm that manufactures *wire coat hangers*. We are a very successful manufacturer of *wire coat hangers*—so successful in recent years that we've just been purchased by a major conglomerate and have the confidence and backing of our parent firm. I have warehouses full of *wire coat hangers*. The problem is that the plastics people have invented an excellent and less expensive coat hanger and I'm having extreme difficulty selling any *wire coat hangers*.

I would greatly appreciate your taking three minutes *right now* and list on a sheet of paper or in the study guide everything you might suggest I do with my *wire coat hangers*—other than hang up clothes. Start now and take three minutes. Please time yourself.

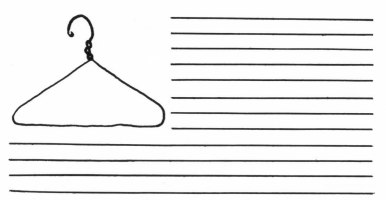

Time—isn't it amazing how long three minutes can be? Now total up the number of ideas you wrote down and write the number on page 25 for further reference. For most of the groups we work with in corporations and associations the average is usually about four or five with a range from 0 to 17.

Now let me ask what can you *not* do with a wire coat hanger? Below are a few examples of answers we have received over the past few years:

Eat it
Wear it
Brush teeth with it
Drive it

All of these are logical and, based upon real life experience, factual answers—but let's look further:

Can't *eat it*—how about: eat *with* it—fork, knife, spoon, . . .

                                       cook *with it*—pot, pan, stove, spatula, . . .

can *with it*—bottle caps, tin cans, . . .

and on—and on—and on

Can't *wear it*—how about: necklaces, belt buckles, garter snaps, earrings, chain mail, shoe nails, steel toed shoes, . . .

We won't belabor the point because we think you know where we're going—you can make out of wire coat hangers, anything which can be made out of metal.

Now don't cry foul too loudly—until you reread the instructions for Practice #1. You'll now probably notice that there were no printed limitations in the instructions—all the limitations on your ability to think creatively came from within based upon your reading "wire coat hanger" five times (perhaps the italics helped just a bit) plus the picture. A picture plus five repetitions is usually enough to functionally fix most people. Could this functional fixation possibly exist in other areas of our lives? You bet!

Breaking this "fun fix" is perhaps the single most important aspect of learning how to approach the future creatively and innovatively solve problems.

To get a handle on opening up the creative genius in each of us let us now take a look at the basic processes of thought and how we develop "the fun fix."

The thought process is composed of three basic components—Knowlege/Imagination/Evaluation. Almost all problem solving we do uses all three in rapid succession and almost in unison. This attempt to tap our wealth of stored knowledge (history), come up with bright, new ideas, and evaluate really creates a schizophrenic double bind; that is, a no win situation. We've been *taught* what is possible just as we've all been *taught* what is absurd (did you ever try to eat a coat hanger—pass the salt).

We've italicized *taught* because most mental processes are

learned. Let us take a look at the educational experience—say from kindergarten to 12th grade. Remember that thought is made up of knowledge, imagination and evaluation; how often in those twelve years of school were you ever asked for a new idea. Make your own pie graph in the study guide or below by drawing a slice of pie and writing the percentage of your "in school" time spent coming up with *new* ideas.

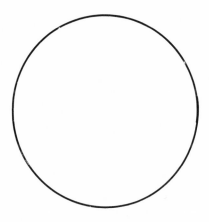

Was your slice small? A friend of mine put down 5 per cent and told me it was usually during recess. Now consider *evaluation.* During your school years did you ever really evaluate the *knowledge* you were taught—no? Well then you could only practice evaluation on the new ideas (were they good, bad, legal, practical . . .) but since so little time was spent coming up with new ideas, most people have little experience in effectively evaluating the few new ideas they do come up with. Now your pie chart probably will look like this:

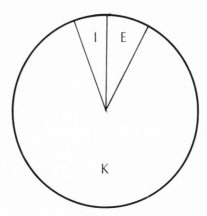

Without reducing our base of knowledge the goal of this book is to show more effective methods for expanding our abilities in the area of Imagination and Evaluation. If you're on the fast track move on to chapter three.

This concentration on learning "what is" and how to use what we've got in "normal" ways is an essential component of the socialization process. Without this wide base of common knowledge it would be very difficult for a consumer based economy to function smoothly.

A world renowned futurist, Dr. George Land, demonstrated this functional fixation very dramatically while working as a consultant to NASA. Dr. Land assembled a group of engineers in a conference or meeting room in which there was a table full of tools and a programmable calculator in addition to the normal pencils, paper, blackboard, etc. In the front of the room on the floor was a steel plate onto which was welded a 30 inch tall pipe about 1½ inches in diameter. Dr. Land placed an ordinary ping pong ball in the upright pipe. He then told the scientists and engineers that he had only one task for them to perform, which was—using anything in the room—to remove the ping pong ball from the pipe without turning it upside down.

The well-educated engineers approached the task with confidence. After a few hours of frustrating effort the group gave up. They had tried every tool available without success. They had developed several mathematical formulas without success. In desperation they even lined up and blew across the top of the pipe in an effort to create a venturi to suck the ball out. At this point Dr. Land had the engineers (adults) sit down and relax and he brought in a group of five year olds. The children were given the problem with the same instructions. Several of the five year olds went to the table full of tools but couldn't figure out how to work any. Several other five year olds went up to write on the chalk board only to find that the engineers had broken all the chalk. One industrious tyke tried to get his hand down the pipe, but that didn't work so they all gathered to discuss the problem. After a brief huddle they each went to a table, picked up the ice water pitcher, poured the water into the pipe and *floated the ball out.*

The engineers cried foul!—"Ice water is for drinking" —and that's functional fixation.

Wishing to further study the "development" of the fun fix, Dr. Land and other researchers at the Turtle Bay Institute in New York in the late 1950's developed a perceptive problem-solving test for five year olds. These tests were administered to a test group of about 1200 children in upstate New York representing a wide cross cultural slice (black, white, Latino—poor, rich, and middle class). After scoring the test the researchers were surprised to find that 92 per cent of those tested scored in the Very Creative category. Perhaps the test was too simple? They decided to continue the longitudinal study as designed. They kept track of the children for five years and administered the test again to ten year olds (the same test—the same children). The results were interesting to say the least—because only 37 per cent of the ten year olds scored as well as 92 per cent had when they were five. The test was continued for another five years. At the age of 15 the same test subjects were given the same test and as high school sophomores only 12 per cent scored in the Very Creative category.

Because of administrative changes and reduction in sample size due to relocations the study was discontinued (perhaps the researchers were also slightly disheartened).

To validate the results against an adult population the same test was given to students at the University of New York at Buffalo. The college students who scored as Very Creative made up only 2 per cent of the total group tested.

Does this study indicate that there is a deterioration of mental processes? No, it does indicate that the classical methods of teaching concentrate on preparing students to *function* in our society. They know how to function for the support of the status quo but are not taught how to constructively change or improve the situation. From our recent educational consulting experiences we see very little change in this pattern for most of the student population. (Many schools have what is called a "young scholars" or gifted student program which teaches creativity. To get into such a gifted program requires a 130 IQ, great grades and scoring in the 98th percentile of any student body—perhaps we're working with the wrong children?)

These may be depressing numbers but do not despair. In each of us there is a five year old just dying to be heard. In almost every adult we have all seen—upon rare occasion—the attempt of the free child to be heard.

In our ego development peers and role models have a very strong influence on how we act and think. For a major portion of society it is the norm that "big boys don't cry" and "good girls don't swear." If you act like your peers and discuss what is acceptable to them you will be "popular." This is part of the normal socialization process and encourages functional fixation.

Another way to say this might be, "He sees things the way I do." In these seven words there is a unbelievable force when we examine holographic memory storage.

Certain researchers contend that memory is the storage of knowledge in *three dimensional form.* In the thought process we can recall knowledge by looking at previous experience. Yes *literally* looking at what happened. If, through education or peer group pressure or whatever, we only look at one side of an issue we are ignoring the holographic (three dimensional) capabilities of our brain. A truly creative person will roll an image around and look at all sides. This can be classed as "putting brain in gear before putting mouth in motion"—a very useful technique in avoiding foot-in-mouth disease.

Rolling an idea, thought or picture around not only allows you to look at all sides but also facilitates recombination of pieces into *new ideas* or creative output. Methods for unlocking creative output will be explored in chapter three.

In the field of psychology it is often useful to know "where a client is coming from," as this relates to his thought patterns and verbal expressions. Recent research by Bandler and Grinder has pinpointed a method which can allow a careful observer to pick up visual cues that indicate what type of thought process is going on at any point in time. For example, if a person were asked a question, the slight redirection of their eyes will tell whether they are dipping into memory (usually visual) or actually making up an answer, which Bandler and Grinder call visual construct. From their research a very useful technique called Neurolinguistic Programming or "NLP" has developed. We've been fortunate enough to have been involved—as a test subject—in videotaping of this NLP process. The test consisted of a set of questions designed to assess visual memory, auditory memory, kinesthetic (feelings) and new images. Although a bit skeptical first, we were amazed when we looked at the videotapes and found each subject responding to each question with predictable eye movements, as if he had a script.

This technique, while very useful in client/therapist relations has monumental potential benefit in the areas of personnel, labor relations and other administrative functions. By "reading" people in conflict related situations we can determine a creative course of action directed at future positive change and growth.

I've recently read a fascinating book by Dr. Eugene T. Grendlin, Ph.D., *Focusing.* (Bantam Books, Inc., 1981) Dr. Grendlin works in the area of clinical psychotherapy and for years has been studying how people solve problems and grow emotionally. One of the main points of his book is something he calls body wisdom. For most people this is a strange concept—until we change the words from body wisdom to—gut feel, woman's intuition or a good hunch. The body wisdom is not as easily accessible as mind wisdom and is often discounted by our evaluation process. How often have you come up with a great idea and didn't "go with your gut feeling?" Your evaluation process rationalized and criticized away a potentially beneficial piece of information.

We've touched upon these various thought concepts to show you that there are many approaches to the thought process—all based on Knowledge/Imagination/Evaluation. These three keys to thought are the basis of all growth with growth being a holistic rather than separatist process. Mentally using everything you've got is the key to future positive decision-making.

We've come a long way from coat hangers—so let's now move on to methods for breaking functional fixation.

chapter three
BREAKING THE PATTERN

Thought habits are sometimes as difficult to break as are such maladaptive habits as smoking or overeating. It takes time and practice to develop new concepts. The key item in expanding creativity, though, is probably the willingness to admit that there might, just possibly, be a better way.

Keep in mind the three basic components of thought: *Knowledge* is what we've learned; *Imagination* is what we can "think up" or "dream up;" and *Evaluation* is our ability to measure the applicability of concepts to the situation at hand.

First, let us look at the role of knowledge in breaking the pattern. Each and every time we add an item of knowledge to our memory we expand the potential for new ideas. New ideas are usually the recombination of existing bits of information—we'll have more on this later. The knowledge pool of each person contains a certain volume of experiences from the mundane to the spectacular. As people mature the brain stores in memory immense quantities of data. Some researchers theorize that each of us has stored in our memory banks every single event which ever occurred to us. The problem occurs in finding ways to retrieve the data in "useable form." Knowledge, as an expanding resource, is always present, even in brain damaged individuals.

The old saying, "If you had half a brain you'd be dangerous," may be an understatement according to a British physician, Dr. John Lorber. As reported in the May 1981 issue of *Science Digest,* Dr. Lorber has extensively studied individuals with hydrocephalus, a disease in which fluids build up in the skull and destroy large portions of the cortex. This is the part of the brain usually given credit for being the center of intelligence or knowledge. Lorber's studies show that among hydrocephalics who lose as much as 95 per cent of their cortex, half have IQ's greater than normal. One interesting patient of Dr. Lorber had a degree with honors in math, and IQ of 126 and had by size, "virtually no brain."

Examples such as this indicate that the storage space available in the normal brain far exceeds our present volume of knowledge needed to be stored. With this tremendous base of knowledge should we ever encounter an unsolvable problem?

This question points in the direction of how this information is stored. If it were stored sequentially as information is stored on computer tapes it would be most difficult to retrieve. If it were stored on computer discs we would need an index to show the access arm where to pick up the information. Many researchers believe the brain stores data in a random, immediate access, holographic fashion.

Immediate random access often occurs during dreaming. The dreams of most people are usually quickly discarded as meaningless because in the awake state the sequence and definition of portions of dreams make little sense. They, at first remembering, do not fit our concept of real or possible.

Could this "unreal" aspect of dreaming reveal our mind's attempt "and ability" to examine all aspects of the dream topic at a single moment?

In the January 1981 issue of *Psychology Today,* Stephen P. LaBerge considers dreams to be "the magic theatre of all possibilities and a workshop of creativity and growth." La-Berge has experimented for over three years in the use of autosuggestion in controlling lucid dreaming. He found dream control not only possible, but also useful in problem solving.

Taking this research one step further we might conclude that if the brain can be directed during sleep—perhaps we can utilize wakeful states much more effectively—and tap the great unused potential.

Recognizing and utilizing the random access three dimensional potential is the first step. This holographic or three dimensional storage of knowledge provides, upon recall, a complete picture of any past (and perhaps future) situations. As an example, take a moment to look at any solid and familiar object in your office. With your eyes you can see the near surface. What does the back of that object look like? Turn the object around in your brain. To test myself on this, I've looked at the solid, fireproof, wooden door to my office. The surface I'm looking at has a door knob and I can see three hinges where it attaches to the door jamb. But what does the back look like? Without moving from my desk I can "picture" the reverse side. It looks almost the same as the near or vision side except for the brass two-pronged coat hook upon which there is a wooden—you guessed it—coat hanger.

Not being superman, I know I don't have x-ray vision; I simply recall past knowledge of what the back of that specific door looks like. The knowledge of this door and many other doors in my life can be quickly recalled.

This pool of knowledge tells us "how things are" but not

"how things might be." It is our *imagination* which provides the potential for change. If everything in our life were perfect we would probably want to stay in a comfortable rut and change nothing—but in any situation calling for a decision or the solution to a problem we need to tap the imagination. The creative imagination can recombine existing pieces of knowledge to form new ideas. But, I could simply tap my memory and solve the problem, or make the decision, the same way I did the last time. Had that worked, why is the same problem popping up again? Perhaps there is a better solution.

Utilizing the imagination and stimulating memory recall can be aided by many simple and time efficient techniques. Let me stress the word simple! Each of the following techniques does not require a Ph.D. in advanced creativity. Within each of us is a creative five year old who will produce if given the opportunity.

Initial attempts to unlock functional fixation and break a thought pattern can be fun and, as you experiment in this area, you may find that new ideas which at first may be quite humorous are the key to a big payoff. Many great inventions were funny, silly, unusual or unbelievable when first conceived (electric light, radio, telephone, airplanes, man on the moon . . .). The initial ideas for these inventions were scoffed at by most people until, with a great deal of effort, their inventors came up with the right combination for success.

There are many methods which can be used to assist in generating creative ideas which can be used to solve problems or identify all the potential options associated with any given situation. These methods can be called *idea triggers* or mind openers.

The mind openers list below is not complete. Also it is not always necessary to use every method every time you need to generate ideas. Often two or three triggers will be sufficient to get the creative juices flowing:

Idea triggers:
   Analogies
   Exaggerations
   Fragmentation
   Free association
   Ideals
   Knowns
     rights
     wrongs
   Minimize
   Mirror image
   Most expensive solution
   Most impractical solution
   New point of entry
   Reversal
     parts
     roles

In discussing each of these individually, keep in mind that it is *not* our goal at this point to generate *good* ideas or solutions. The purpose of mind triggers is simply to *generate ideas!* Evaluation of the ideas will come later. Each of these triggers is a way to roll an idea around and look at the other side. With holographic memory storage this is a simple process.

We'll give you, below, a brief explanation of each of the triggers. Each of the concepts, given only a paragraph here, could easily be expanded to a full chapter. These are listed alphabetically and not in order of importance. Which is most useful will be determined by the specific situation in which you choose to use them.

ANALOGIES: Through the use of analogies an individual can remove himself from the hot seat and take a remote view of a situation. This release of pressure often allows new potential solutions to surface. The method is to make up a story about a problem which is similar to your problem. In the story solve the *other* problem and you might find the key to solving your own problem.

EXAGGERATION: Make the problem or decision so huge that it will take an act of Congress to solve it. Blowing things totally out of proportion can often generate positive stress which will unlock the functional fixation and provide direction toward a solution.

FRAGMENTATION: Break up a problem into pieces. A good example is writing a book—considered by most people to be an impossible task—but anyone can write a word, sentence, paragraph, chapter and maybe even a book. Fragmentation or segmentation narrows the scope of any task and allows for concentration of energy.

FREE ASSOCIATION: Also called brainstorming, this can generate some truly outlandish ideas which could turn out to be the best problem solutions to cash in on free association. Whenever some creative people are working on a paper, report, or book, they keep two pads of paper on their desk—the one they are working on plus a blank upon which they'll scribble "free" ideas which pop up as they are working. Most of this "mind chatter" will be thrown out later, but it always contains a good idea or two which would have disappeared had they not been written down. Also, by writing the "free" ideas down, the mind is kept clear and can concentrate on the first priority project being worked on.

IDEALS: Ideals are nice, but who can afford them? When looking for a better solution write any and all ideals without regard to self or organizationally imposed restraints—don't evaluate, just generate ideal solutions.

KNOWNS: How much do you presently know about a situation? Knowns fall into two categories: the things that are right and the things that are wrong. Make two lists and be sure to include everything—even things such as, "My mother likes it," or "My Uncle George had one in 1947." Seemingly irrelevant data can be useful.

MINIMIZE: By shrinking a problem and placing it in a global perspective you can picture what other facts, people, or events will influence what has happened, is going on, or will occur. The process of minimizing is similar to fragmentation except that fragmentation deals with just a small part of a problem, minimizing with the whole problem.

MIRROR IMAGE: Most people can comb their hair or tie a tie in a mirror. Some day you should try to try on a pair of shoes while looking in a mirror, or tie someone else's tie. We all develop motor coordination habits, and attempting the mirror challenge can be unnerving. Familiar objects look and feel differently. The mind will treat a mirror image quite differently than it will treat the real thing—especially if the real thing is an old and tough problem which the mind is *stuck* on.

MOST EXPENSIVE SOLUTION: Most managers are concerned with budget controls and bottom line. If they get a chance to have carte blanche their minds will usually explode with ideas once the financial constraints are released. Back in the early '70's when the occupational safety laws (OSHA) were enacted, there was a distribution center manager in Minnesota. His warehouse had a mezzanine with a railing but no toeboard to prevent tools or other objects from being kicked down on to the people working below. This was in violation of the OSHA Law. The corporate architects designed a super system of welded steel screens which would have cost over $7,000. After looking at the blue prints of the *most expensive* solution the manager dropped his pencil—it rolled and stopped against the wall of his office. He picked it up and looked again at the blue prints labeled *mezzanine toeboard.* The word toeboard finally sunk in. (Look at the wall near where you sit—does the wall go all the way to the floor or is there a "toeboard" in your office?) As a team the architects designed a *most expensive* solution which pointed out to the operations manager (thanks to dropping a pencil) the fact that he could solve the problem with $176.00 worth of 2 X 4's, pipe clamps and one-inch roundhead screws. As I remember he did receive maximum bonus that year.

MOST IMPRACTICAL SOLUTION: This can be almost as much fun as the most expensive. Take your problem and write down crazy, impractical solutions—after you get those out of the way you can go full steam ahead on the right solution. Practicality is a great limiter in creativity. An example might be the cement boat. Crazy! But cement doesn't rot or rust and a faro-cement sail boat is heavy and very stable. Can you see the expressions on the faces of a group of marine architects when trying to decide on the proper material for a hull when the group clown said, "Hell, we'll use cement."

NEW POINT OF ENTRY: Not either the front door or back door but through the window. Years ago when coal furnaces were common in houses the coal chute was through the basement window. If administration is having difficulty with a problem perhaps a new point of entry, nursing or maintenance or accounting might provide the solution.

REVERSAL: In most situations there are numerous people or parts so reversal can apply to juxtaposition of parts or role reversal. Once on assignment in Toronto a U.S. based consultant was having great difficulty explaining to the computer center supervisor just how he wanted the data input verified. He took off his suit coat, had the supervisor put it on, and had her explain to him how it should be done while he gave the objections. The problem was solved in three minutes.

These examples of idea triggers can be applied to many situations. The key to their success is not to destroy their effectiveness by inserting evaluation in the middle. Imagination or idea generation must be allowed to proceed unencumbered by evaluation. Never ask or expect good ideas—just ideas—determine their worth later.

A good illustration of this three dimensional process can be found in an ordinary water faucet.

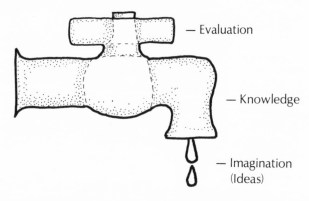

— Evaluation

— Knowledge

— Imagination (Ideas)

The pipe coming out of the wall is the source (Knowledge); the valve regulates the flow (Evaluation) of the water (Ideas). If you were thirsty, wanted a drink and turned the valve, water would flow. If water came out rusty—what would you do? Most people would let the rusty water flow believing clean water to be close behind. Why is it that when most people turn on the brain valve and get a bit of rust (a not so good idea) they immediately close the valve and cut off the flow of all ideas, trapping the rust inside. The key to creativity is to leave the valve open and generate all ideas. With water we catch it in a glass for later evaluation and use. With ideas we catch them on paper for later evaluation and use.

Every idea is a legitimate idea when being creative.

At the beginning of chapter two we conducted an experiment with a wire coat hanger. To measure progress let us now measure—for three minutes—your new and expanded creative ability.

Practice #2 instructions

The situation is this: I need your help. I am the president of a firm which manufactures *leather belts.* We are a very successful manufacturer of *leather belts*—so successful in recent years that we have just been purchased by a major conglomerate and have the backing and confidence of our new parent firm. I have warehouses full of *leather belts* and unlimited resources. The problem is that people have switched to elastic waist bands and I'm having extreme difficulty selling *leather belts* to hold up pants.

Take three minutes—right now—and list anything you can think of that I might do with my belts other than to hold up pants. Use the study guide or the space below.

(George Land's favorite idea was to sew them together and make a new cow.) Here we go—three minutes:

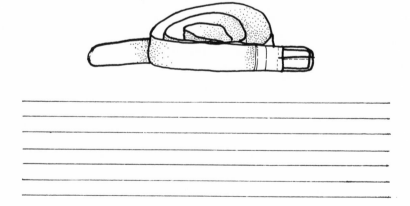

Time's up! When the mind is creating, time can pass very quickly. Total up your number of ideas.

Now return to page 6; the coat hanger total was _____. Your creative ability has increased _____ per cent. Congratulations.

For many people using the imagination *without* evaluation is a difficult task, which will take practice. I encourage people to practice at least three times a week just to keep the creative juices flowing. How many times have you been eating breakfast and found youself reading the Grape Nuts box because the paper hasn't arrived? Rather than read the cereal box—which you've probably already memorized—keep an 8½ X 11 pad and pencil in the kitchen. Use a three minute egg timer and write down new uses for—the oven, the clock, a spoon, the microwave, the toaster . . . You might even come up with a new time saving device for the kitchen of the two career family. NOTE: Be sure to destroy your sheet of ideas before your spouse or children see it—they'll think you've been working too hard!

chapter four
DIVERGENT THOUGHT

The Creative Decision-Making process begins with the generation of ideas. This can be called Divergent Thought. The concept is to diverge, open up, and allow the mind to generate ideas. Remember: don't look for good, or new, or acceptable ideas—just ideas!

The person generating ideas simply starts with a blank sheet of paper to write down all of his or her ideas. These ideas need not be connected or related, or they can follow a pattern. Either way. The most productive idea generators will tap an inner sense, which I call mind chatter. Free association, purge, brainstorm allows the mind the luxury of operating without the strait-jacket of evaluation.

This individual process also can be engaged in via a group setting. We will examine that approach later on in this book. Now let's concentrate on the individual.

Depending upon the complexity of the problem or decision, the mental purge could take as little as 15 or 20 minutes or as long as one or two hours.

I hear you loud and clear. *What the devil do we generate ideas about (other than coat hangers or belts)?* In any decision-making or problem-solving situation there must be a "stated situation which you hope to improve" through the use of some resource. I define resource as what you've got, i.e. time, money, manpower, etc. Also a resource is anything you can get—which includes everything in the world (remember we're in the purge—we'll get practical *later*).

This is an extremely broad definition and it must be broad for a stated purpose. Broad signifies decision-making latitude —space to function—space to grow. Too often time is wasted attempting to define a specific problem and boil it down to the point of solution—possibly ignoring good, the best or most efficient solution. By keeping the problem broad we can avoid the pitfalls of evaluation entering in the purge at this very early stage.

Examples of *general* problems might include:

- How can I improve morale?
- How can I improve productivity?
- Where should I locate our next factory?
- How can Emergency Room service be improved?
- What new car should I buy?
- Which school would be best for my high school senior?
- Which vegetables should I plant this year?
- Where should the family go on vacation?
- What course should I take in night school?

As you can see, this process is applicable to almost any decision-making situation from a multi-million dollar factory to a family vacation site choice. By limiting the problem, you might also limit the solution.

Start your individual purge by listing all the things you can think of that are wrong with the present situation.

If your stated goal is, "How can I improve productivity?" the wrongs might be elicited by saying, "What is wrong with, or what causes present productivity?" The *bad!*

A list such as the following might be generated:
Stink, too low, unprofitable, sick leave, coffee breaks, tardiness, poor quality, time clocks, customer complaints, service problems, poor supervision, training problems, turnover, recruiting, variable from day to day, variable by the hour, large interplant differences, seasonal fluctuations. . . .
Use as many sheets of paper as is necessary. There's probably a great deal of rust listed above which needed to be cleared out of the way. Next, list everything that is good about present productivity. Items such as:
Meets seasonal demands, can be quickly expanded with overtime, can handle small jobs, simple machine conversion, very little union influence, no feather bedding, pride in workmanship, limited turnover, middle age workforce, seasonal, flexible . . .
As you probably noticed, some of the ideas in the *good* area directly contradict items in the *bad* section. This always occurs—even when an individual is doing a single purge. (In a group process purge, the ability of the group to look at items from different angles or from a different perspective, different shift, different background or different expectation level can enhance the volume of ideas.)

You have probably also noticed duplication. This should not be discouraged. *Write it all down.* Looking for duplicates can stifle the flow. "Have I said that before," is a form of evaluation. Don't worry about spellings, abbreviations, or hidden meanings; just write the essence of each idea. Each section (bads, goods . . .) will start slowly and build in output—each idea triggering another. Keep a section going until things really slow down or stop. If you've finished the bads and are working on the goods, and you think up another bad, go over to a bad sheet and write it down.

Now that the bads and goods of the present situation have been dumped on paper, the pathways of the brain are clean enough to begin listing ideal solutions. (Or shall I say "potential" ideal solutions.)

Some productivity ideal potentials might be:

Piece work, quality circles, flexible time, assembly teams, cottage industries, cross training, inservice education, on the job training (OJT), supervisor bonus, worker bonus, assemble name on products, cradle to grave employment, a company picnic, job rotation, expanded benefits, an employee assistance program, relaxation breaks, health breaks, all employee assistance program, relaxation breaks, health breaks, all employees exempt, company paid union dues, a company health spa, better medical insurance, a company Jazzercize program, a para course, health education, psychological counseling, brainwashing, big brother, drugs, fresh fruit free, carpeted floors, work station chairs, robots, R2D2, music, shorter shifts, a four day week, seven-on-seven-off, company housing, company car pool, employee of the month, perfect attendance awards ($ or ?), no smoking, free cigarettes, wine with lunch, birthday parties, birthday off, shift choice, showers, locker room, employee lounge, new lights, uniforms, company store, group discounts, a credit union, clean rest rooms, air conditioning, a company shrink, stress breaks, a swimming pool, scholarships for employees' kids, an essay contest, certify a union, decertify the union, suggestion box, awards for best suggestion . . .

As you can see, this list of ideal solutions could go on for quite some time. (I wrote this on a very bumpy United Airlines flight to Salt Lake City; with a group, a larger number of ideas could be generated.)

Some of these ideas are silly—some are grandiose—some might even be—perish the thought—practical.

The fascinating thing about the purge is that the three lists we've compiled contain ideas, raw, not yet evaluated, *ideas!* Within these lists lies the solution to our productivity problem. These lists we'll call the basic three. Depending upon your comfort level with the situation and how well the purge is going, you may wish to stop here—or you could make additional lists based upon the other mind opening, creativity based concepts discussed in the previous chapter on breaking your "fun fix." To implement all of these productivity improvement ideas is beyond comprehension, even for Congress with our tax dollars for support, so now the task is to refine the massive purge lists and develop a workable set of objectives—a process called Convergent (bringing together) Thought. That's the subject of our next chapter.

All the people who read this may not be in a position to properly associate or relate to productivity. With this in mind, we've developed two additional examples of the purge process showing its applicability in divergent situations.

In the first let's deal with a nationwide or global problem. The question: How can we improve the health of man (physical/emotional/spiritual)? Any group or individual could be considered appropriate for this one.

First the wrongs (or bads):

Deteriorating, counter-productive, healer oriented, passive, wait and see, expensive, disease oriented, multifaceted, fragmented, insurance, doctors, smoking, booze, diseases, undefinable, unmanageable, no concern of mine, no faith, drugs, symptom oriented, old age, exercise, diet, western medicine, doctor knows best, expensive, no use trying, people don't care, insurance will pay, medicare, AMA, dentists, children, stress, overweight, pollution, chemicals, additives . . .

Now add your own below or on a sheet of paper:

_____

_____

Next consider all the things that are *right* with health:
Fun, long life, fewer diseases, technology, hospitals, exercise, no smoking, good food, faith, stress management, doctors, transplants, physical therapy, intensive care units, paramedics, drugs, education, psychology, therapy, psychiatry, vacations, holidays, research, vaccines, insurance, concern, research, human potential, nurses, dentists, headache clinics, TV educational programs for kids, annual physicals . . .

Now add your own below or on a sheet of paper:

Again we have some items in both lists. Without evaluation (remember we have unlimited resources and anything is possible) we'll make a list of ideals of health and how to attain it:
No sickness, personal harmony, balance, free health care, more doctors, shorter hospital stays, health spas, unlimited sick pay, no sick pay, life long health education, health pay, personal responsibility, a health plan, holistic medicine, hospice for dying, more exercise, no food additives, TV health education, library health programs, nurse educators in every town and neighborhood, barefoot doctors, eliminate pollution, ban cigarettes, cure the common cold, a health club in every company, more school health education, free vitamins . . .
Now add your own ideas below or on a sheet of paper:

When doing a purge, sometimes people will blurt out an idea and have no memory of the source of that "new idea". Thank the powers that be—and accept the inspiration. At this point we only want *all ideas*—evaluation comes later. Trying to find the source of an idea can slow the flow.

Another example could revolve around the concept of continuing education or personal growth. The lead question might be, "What additional education do I need?" or "What should I study?" Rather than ask what's wrong with my present knowledge, rephrase the question to ask what don't I know enough about—and purge:

Anthropology, sex, psychology, lumber, chicken farming, welding, business management, assertiveness, salesmanship, law, gastroenterology, genetics, political science . . .

Now add your ideas below or on a sheet of paper:

_____

_____

Now list areas in which I know a fair amount:

Business management, public speaking, organic gardening, parent effectiveness, gestalt psychotherapy, automobile repair, employee assistance programs, nurse recruiting, warehousing, distribution, computer order entry, bricklaying . . .

Now add your own ideas below or on a sheet of paper:

_____

_____

Now generate a list of ideals—no restraints—no holes barred, topics such as:

Space flight, solar energy, politics, futures trading, race car driving, hard rock gold mining, kite flying, hot air ballooning, gliding, soaring, altered mind states, parapsychology, law . . .

Now add your ideas below or on a sheet of paper:

_____

_____

Certain individuals will include items in purge lists which, no matter what the topic, will be the same. This phenomenon simply reflects strong personal bias and depending upon the problem at hand or the topic being considered will be considered "rusty water" or "the true meat of the issue." Even the casual observer has noticed certain people in groups always have "their own ax to grind." The purge process allows for non-detrimental grinding. Purging is non-judgmental and encourages any and all ideas. By recognizing these ideas (writing them down) we defuse potential interpersonal conflicts and get down on the bottom line of making decisions and solving problems. (More on the group process appears in chapter ten).

Any individual can become proficient at generating ideas, with practice. As I mentioned at the end of chapter three, you'll be amazed by the large number of optional uses most items have and the large number of potential solutions to most problems. All it takes is a bit of practice to draw them out of yourself.

When you practice be sure that you don't leave your purge lists laying around. Truly creative lists, when read by the uneducated, casual observer, will lead them to think you're either senile or schizophrenic. Also, the judge at your sanity hearing may not have had the opportunity to read this book.

Divergent thought—allowing the mind to clear—encouraging digression—generating ideas—the purge is, in surgical terms, clearing the operating field for action.

chapter five
CONVERGENT THOUGHT

According to Webster's New Collegiate Dictionary: "CONVERGE 1: to tend or move toward one point or one another: come together: MEET 2: to come together and unite in a common interest or focus 3: to approach a limit as the number of terms increases without limit: to cause to converge."

In previous chapters we kept the topic of discussion fairly open and broad, not attempting to limit our options. In the process of convergent thought—individual or group—the direction is to refine and bring together in a common interest or focus.

When moving from a purge (Divergent Thought) to Convergent Thought (Objective Setting) it is often beneficial to rephrase the initial question and narrow the focus. In chapter four, the first sample purge was on productivity, In rephrasing we could put the hoped-for decision in the following terms: How can I improve the productivity of the production workers in the third shift of the XYZ Birdhouse Manufacturing Plant? Or with the health example: What items can we expect to positively impact the health of the employees here at Community Memorial Hospital?

In psychological terms you might say we are beginning to move from periphery toward core—from cocktail chatter to real conversation. This process is relatively simple after the purge because of the reduction in tension enhanced by the lists of *ideas.* We might believe the correct answer to the stated problem is right there in front of us—let's pick it out.

There are two basic ways to go. If you are serving as a group leader or doing this yourself, the purge lists can be refined to a specific number of objectives (say 10 or 20) or you can pick an undetermined number from 10 to whatever. A word of caution; below ten items will greatly limit your options and above twenty or so becomes a laborious mechanical process.

The individual working the process will usually *set* a number of potential objectives at the start. In teaching the process we always use ten objectives because of speed and simplicity (plus the fact that we've already pre-printed the ten parameter work sheets). When consulting with an organization on a specific problem we'll use 20. Twenty gives a more complete picture (and again the work sheets are pre-printed). In chapters six and seven the worksheets are discussed in detail.

The convergent process begins with the statement: "Now that I've listed all of the ideas I will select from these lists the ten (12, 15, 17, N) ideas which best fit the problem at hand. By reviewing the lists, the ideas with potential payback can be selected and written down in *any* order on the objective list. (When reviewing the purge lists you are not yet doing hard evaluation. Don't discuss the "why" or "how much" of any item. Don't rationalize. At this stage any idea is still only an idea—also the ideas are not limited to those on the purge list. If you generate a new one—write it down.)

All of the items written on the objective list should be stated in a positive manner (i.e., if you feel that "lack of team spirit" is affecting productivity write it in the objective list as "esprit de corps.") From the purge lists ideals can often be directly picked up, but wrongs or bads need to be rephrased or flipped into the positive.

Do *not* get trapped by evaluation. Normal everyday evaluation is based upon history and this decision making process is *future* oriented. Beware of evaluative thoughts or concepts such as:

That will never work . . .

Our company is too small for that . . .

We have a union here . . .

Can't afford that . . .

Mother told me I shouldn't . . .

Government red tape . . .

Insurance companies will scream . . .

We've left room for your organization's favorite excuse or "reason" for killing ideas. Jot them down above or use a sheet of paper. You'll notice again that we simply said *ideas,* not good ideas, but simply *ideas* relative to the problem at hand. All too often *ideas* are killed or put on the back burner before we have a chance to decide which are good or not so good.

The ideas you list can (and probably will) be unrelated. Some may be very similar. Don't worry about a totally ridiculous idea that somehow got on the list. If it is truly bad it will drop out during evaluation.

Now let's set ten objectives for XYZ productivity. Reviewing the purge in chapter four, we've selected:

XYZ productivity

1) More supervisor training
2) Quality circles
3) Cross training
4) Piece work bonus
5) Flex time
6) Four day week
7) New equipment
8) Air conditioning
9) Employee health spa
10) Child day care

These are *not* in rank order! They are numbered only to facilitate the evaluation process later on. The numbers are "objective reference" numbers.

The ideas listed above are those of the authors. If you as an individual or as part of the XYZ management team were to become involved in the process, you would probably— based upon your unique knowledge and experience—have selected a different combination of objectives.

We have now completed the open minded, relatively unstructured, portion of the process. As mentioned before, the previous two steps can be done as an individual or group process. It is from this point that we can move on to evaluation.

To provide the reader with another example we'll continue with the topic of "improving health specifically for the employees of Community Memorial Hospital." This example could easily be transfered to any other facility (bank, business, union, etc.) As in the previous example we'll turn bads into goods, wrongs into rights, and rights into ideals which will be listed on the objectives list. We've decided to use eighteen objectives and will continue this second example through to completion in the following chapters to give you a point of comparison with the productivity example.

1) Exercise programs
2) Annual physicals
3) Employee assistance program
4) Health education program
5) Employee health spa
6) Health goals (MBO's)
7) Stop smoking clinic
8) Flex time
9) Management commitment
10) Free medication
11) Exercise breaks
12) Biofeedback
13) Health pay
14) Three weeks vacation per year
15) Accumulate sick days
16) Relaxation (meditation breaks)
17) Shorter hours
18) Weight control clinic

Again—these are *not* rank ordered, the numbers are for reference only. You'll notice that by enlarging the number of objectives we've attained greater scope while maintaining manageability. At first glance some of these items don't fit into the concept of cost care containment and some are down right absurd. *Oh!* Excuse us—we promised no evaluation until chapter six.

chapter six
COMPARATIVE VALUATION

While a lot has been written on the art of mind expansion, brainstorming and idea generation, few methods are detailed for effective valuation. Most time-management programs and books teach individuals to rank in order of priority their potential projects for improved time efficiency and minimal waste. One great drawback to all of these methods is the mind's ability to "rationalize away a good idea because of lack of experience with the idea or possibly prejudice based upon some prior experience." Also the highest value item may not be the one with highest payback potential.

To sidestep the "if I'd only" and "we really should" which clutter any decision making process the following multiple regression type of technique is used. As you work through this regression process (for a simpler name, lets call it paired weighting) you will probably say—good grief, this is similar to the personal preference test given by placement counselors or high school guidance counselors. Right you are. Those tests you remember were highly researched and designed to assist people in planning the rest of their lives. The underlying concept is to encourage people to make small nonthreatening decisions—keep the choices simple.

This chapter will deal with the use of this technique of evaluation in any decision making situation. The purpose of paired weighting is to compare each objective or potential area of interest against every other objective once. The number of items used is 100 per cent flexible. In the course we teach at Forest Hospital we use ten items for the sake of simplicity in teaching the process. In most business or consulting situations, we'll use up to twenty objectives to develop a more complete picture of potential high payback areas. From 10 to 20 can be done quickly with pencil and paper. Over 20 is mechanically messy.

In chapter five we made a list of 10 objectives. (As I have already mentioned this list could have contained 12, 15, 19 or any number suitable.) For the sake of speed and simplicity we can construct a worksheet on which we'll compare item #1 with all the other items once. The sheet will look like: $\frac{1\ 1\ 1\ 1\ 1\ 1\ 1\ 1\ 1}{2\ 3\ 4\ 5\ 6\ 7\ 8\ 9\ 10}$. A worksheet such as this relieves us of the tedium of spelling out each choice as is done on most copyrighted selection tests. It is provided in your study guide along with the rest of the charts.

Comparing item number two to each of the other objectives is a similar process *except* that we've already compared #2 and #1 so in this step, #2 will be compared to #3 through #10:

$$\frac{2\ 2\ 2\ 2\ 2\ 2\ 2\ 2}{3\ 4\ 5\ 6\ 7\ 8\ 9\ 10}.$$

Similarly #3 is compared with #4 through #10:

$\frac{3\ 3\ 3\ 3\ 3\ 3\ 3}{4\ 5\ 6\ 7\ 8\ 9\ 10}$ and you continue this process until you have compared the second to last objective to the last item which in this case is #10. (As I mentioned before it can be any number.)

Each successive row will have one less digit until the chart is complete and takes the shape of a right triangle as shown below:

1. _____	$\dfrac{1\ 1\ 1\ 1\ 1\ 1\ 1\ 1\ 1}{2\ 3\ 4\ 5\ 6\ 7\ 8\ 9\ 10}$	
2. _____	$\dfrac{2\ 2\ 2\ 2\ 2\ 2\ 2\ 2}{3\ 4\ 5\ 6\ 7\ 8\ 9\ 10}$	
3. _____	$\dfrac{3\ 3\ 3\ 3\ 3\ 3\ 3}{4\ 5\ 6\ 7\ 8\ 9\ 10}$	
4. _____	$\dfrac{4\ 4\ 4\ 4\ 4\ 4}{5\ 6\ 7\ 8\ 9\ 10}$	
5. _____	$\dfrac{5\ 5\ 5\ 5\ 5}{6\ 7\ 8\ 9\ 10}$	
6. _____	$\dfrac{6\ 6\ 6\ 6}{7\ 8\ 9\ 10}$	
7. _____	$\dfrac{7\ 7\ 7}{8\ 9\ 10}$	
8. _____	$\dfrac{8\ 8}{9\ 10}$	
9. _____	$\dfrac{9}{10}$	
10. _____	____	

If you wish to take the time you can count up how often each number is represented. (It's 9.) With this chart each objective represented by a number is given equal opportunity to have a high or low value. Notice we moved the ten productivity objectives from chapter five to the numbered lines to the left of the working chart. (Any sequence will do.)

Previously, we mentioned that we were going to compare each item with every other item *once*. This is done by asking yourself the key question: "If I could have equal parts of number one or number two, which would I like a little more of," or "which one is slightly more important?" This is not an either/or situation. Since you know you can have both— you can quickly make the decision. Using the following work sheet or the one in the study guide, with the objectives carried forward from the previous chapter mark your choice by *circling,* in red, the number you chose—either #1 or #2. The reason we suggest red is because we are using black and you can, in chapter eight, see if you agree with the authors on any points. Now using the same question, compare #1 to #3—circle your choice, #1 to #4—circle your choice, and so on until you have 9 circles across the top of the work page. It is important that you make a choice for each and every possibility and always work from left to right. Don't agonize over the decision because if you think about any of these long enough you can rationalize away a good idea. Make the decision quickly and move on to the next.

Now move down to line two and compare objective #2 with #3 using the same question. Continue with #2/#4, #2/#5, #2/#6 and so on until you finish the line.

		Value	%
1. Supervisor training	① ① ① 1 1 ① 1 ① 1 2 3 4 ⑤ ⑥ 7 ⑧ 9⑩	1 =	5
2. Quality circles	2 ② 2 ② ② 2 ② ② ③ 4 ⑤ 6 7 ⑧ 9 10	2 =	5
3. Cross training	③ 3 ③ ③ ③ ③ ③ 4 ⑤ 6 7 8 9 10	3 =	7
4. Piece work bonuses	4 4 ④ ④ ④ ④ ⑤ ⑥ 7 8 9 10	4 =	4
5. Flex time	⑤ ⑤ 5 ⑤ 5 6 7 ⑧ 9⑩	5 =	7
6. Four day week	⑥ 6 ⑥ 6 7 ⑧ 9⑩	6 =	4
7. New equipment	7 ⑦ 7 ⑧ 9⑩	7 =	1
8. Air conditioning	⑧ ⑧ 9 10	8 =	7
9. Employee health spa	9 ⑩	9 =	O
10. Child day care		10 =	5

Having completed this process you've made 90 comparisons resulting in 45 decisions. The first time through this process can take 10 or 15 minutes, but with practice you'll be able to make 45 decisions on any subject in less than 5 minutes. (It's so quick that if we don't like the numbers we've got plenty of time to do it again—more about this later.)

Now for the most difficult part of the entire process. It's called counting circles—don't laugh because most people goof up this part. The #1's are simple. Count the number of times you circled #1 in red and check off each circle as you count. Our total (black) in this example is 5 which we will write in on the line to the right of the first objective or the number one item. Enter your red total in the study guide.

Next, count the number of times the #2's on the page have been circled. Starting in the *top* row, go down and then across left to right checking off the number two's.

Next count the number three's—start in the *top* row, go down and across. (Some people have said count in an L shape—down and to the right.)

Continue this process until you counted all the red circles for each number and recorded your value for each number on the appropriate objective line. After all the values are entered, total this column and, with ten objectives, the total should be 45. (With twenty objectives the total would be 190.)

Using this process any individual can quickly put down, with a high degree of accuracy, exactly how they rank or value any group of items.

This completes the comparative valuation process. Below are additional examples and a practice sheet. If you're following the fast track move to chapter seven.

Examples and practice
Example #1

Assuming the management of Community Memorial has selected eighteen objectives from the original purge (as has been done in chapter five), we will need to construct an 18 objective paired weighting worksheet. The design is exactly the same as a 10 parameter sheet except slightly larger. On this larger sheet the objectives will no longer fit alongside the "triangle" so we'll insert them here.

1) Exercise program
2) Annual physicals
3) Employee assistance program
4) Health ed program
5) Employee health spa
6) Health goals (MBO's)
7) Stop smoking clinic
8) Flex time
9) Management commitment
10) Free medication
11) Exercise breaks
12) Biofeedback
13) Health pay
14) Three week vacation per year
15) Accumulate sick days
16) Relaxation breaks
17) Shorter hours
18) Weight control clinic

You might notice that several of these objectives are also listed under Productivity in the fast track. This reflects the feelings of both authors regarding the relationship between Health and Productivity.

We have made our choices (in black) on the worksheet in the study guide and on page 47 responding to the same basic questions used in the fast track Productivity example: "If I could have equal parts of #1—exercise program or #2—physicals, which could I like just a little bit more of?" Enter your valuation using a different color ink on the same worksheet—but try not to be influenced by our responses. (In example #2 we'll provide a blank worksheet.)

$$\frac{①\ ①\ 1\ ①\ 1\ ①\ 1\ ①\ 1\ ①\ ①\ 1\ ①\ ①\ ①\ ①}{2\ \ 3\ ④\ 5\ ⑥\ 7\ ⑧⑨10⑪12\ 13⑭15\ 16\ 17\ 18} \quad 11$$

$$\frac{2\ 2\ 2\ 2\ 2\ 2\ 2\ ②\ 2\ 2\ ②\ 2\ ②\ 2\ ②\ 2}{③\ ④\ ⑤\ ⑥\ ⑦\ ⑧\ ⑨10⑪⑫13⑭15⑯17⑱} \quad 4$$

$$\frac{3\ ③\ 3\ 3\ ③\ 3\ ③\ 3\ ③③③③\ 3\ ③\ 3}{④\ 5\ ⑥⑦\ 8\ ⑨10\ ⑪12\ 13\ 14\ 15⑯17\ ⑱} \quad 9$$

$$\frac{④\ 4\ ④④\ 4\ ④④④④④④④④④\ 4}{5\ ⑥\ 7\ 8\ ⑨10\ 11\ 12\ 13\ 14\ 15\ 16\ 17⑱} \quad 14$$

$$\frac{5\ 5\ ⑤\ 5\ ⑤⑤⑤⑤\ 5\ ⑤\ 5\ ⑤⑤}{⑥⑦\ 8\ ⑨10\ 11\ 12\ 13⑭15⑯17\ 18} \quad 9$$

$$\frac{⑥⑥\ 6\ ⑥⑥⑥⑥\ 6\ ⑥\ 6\ ⑥⑥}{7\ 8\ ⑨10\ 11\ 12\ 13⑭15⑯17\ 18} \quad 14$$

$$\frac{7\ 7\ ⑦⑦⑦\ 7\ ⑦\ 7\ ⑦⑦}{⑧\ ⑨10\ 11\ 12\ 13\ ⑭15\ ⑯17\ 18} \quad 10$$

$$\frac{8\ ⑧\ 8\ ⑧⑧\ 8\ ⑧⑧⑧⑧}{⑨10⑪12\ 13⑭15\ 16\ 17\ 18} \quad 10$$

$$\frac{⑨⑨⑨⑨\ 9\ ⑨\ 9\ ⑨⑨}{10\ 11\ 12\ 13⑭15\ ⑯17\ 18} \quad 15$$

$$\frac{10\ 10\ 10\ 10\ 10\ 10\ 10\ 10\ 10}{⑪⑫⑬⑭⑮⑯⑰⑱} \quad 0$$

$$\frac{⑪⑪\ 11\ ⑪\ 11\ ⑪\ 11}{12\ 13\ ⑭15\ ⑯17\ ⑱} \quad 9$$

$$\frac{⑫\ 12\ 12\ 12\ ⑫\ 12}{13⑭⑮⑯17\ ⑱} \quad 4$$

$$\frac{13\ 13\ 13\ ⑬\ 13}{⑭⑮\ ⑯17\ ⑱} \quad 2$$

$$\frac{⑭⑭⑭⑭}{15\ 16\ 17\ 18} \quad 15$$

$$\frac{15\ ⑮\ 15}{⑯17\ ⑱} \quad 4$$

$$\frac{⑯⑯}{17\ 18} \quad 13$$

$$\frac{17}{⑱} \quad 1$$

$$9$$

As with the productivity example the most confusing part of the process is counting the circles. Count each number in your personal color of ink and enter the total value in the value column on the right, adjacent to our values. The first row (#1's) count from left to right. In every other row use the "L" shaped counting method starting from the top and go down the column and then across the row. i.e., to count the value for #5 you would start in the top row with $\frac{1}{5}$, move down to $\frac{2}{5}$, then $\frac{3}{5}$, $\frac{4}{5}$; then from left to right $\frac{5\ 5\ 5\ 5\ 5}{6\ 7\ 8\ 9\ 10,} \ldots \frac{5}{18,}$ counting each time you circled the #5. The correct number of black circles around a 5 is 9. The number of circled 5's in your color ink is probably different.

As you are by now fully aware, in this health example we have only eight more objectives than in the productivity example, but we have more than tripled the number of choices to be made. The value column check digit is 153.

Example #2 is included at this point to provide additional practice on a topic totally apart from business (unless you're a truck farmer).

If you have a vegetable garden every year, *but* you're never sure which or how much of each to grow, give this a try. Do the purge listing everything you think you might want to grow (a seed catalog would help). The ideals purge list might look like the one on page 49.
From the purge list we can select 10 or 20 objectives. (Keep in mind that you live on a quarter-acre lot and the garden is 20 feet long and three feet wide. (A global view of the situation helps at this stage.)

From this purge list we'll select 12 items which seem most appropriate and list them on a 12 item paired weighting worksheet in the study guide and on page 49.

You'll notice that the process is the same with 12 (or any number) as it is with ten or 18 except the check

Peas	Cauliflower	Dill	Carrots	Corn
Chives	Squash	Tomatoes	Parsley	Pumpkins
Rutabaga	Spinach	Radish	Zucchini	Lettuce
Potatoes	Collards	Cucumbers	Garlic	Gourds
Ground Cherries	Gladiolas	Pole Beans	Asparagus	Strawberries
Green Onions	Lima Beans	Rhubarb	Broccoli	_____
_____	_____	_____	_____	_____
_____	_____	_____	_____	_____

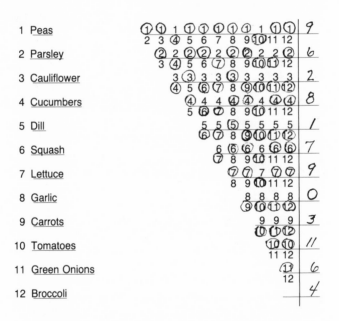

1 Peas

2 Parsley

3 Cauliflower

4 Cucumbers

5 Dill

6 Squash

7 Lettuce

8 Garlic

9 Carrots

10 Tomatoes

11 Green Onions

12 Broccoli

digit changes. With 12 the value column total changes to 66.

We have made our choices and entered our values using black ink in the above example. On page 50 and in the study guide are exact duplicates upon which you can circle (in red) your choices. (If I could have 1. peas or 2. parsley, 1. peas or 3. cauliflower, 1. peas or . . . —which would I prefer?)

1 Peas	
2 Parsley	
3 Cauliflower	
4 Cucumbers	
5 Dill	
6 Squash	
7 Lettuce	
8 Garlic	
9 Carrots	
10 Tomatoes	
11 Green Onions	
12 Broccoli	

```
1  1  1  1  1  1  1  1  1  1  1
2  3  4  5  6  7  8  9 10 11 12
   2  2  2  2  2  2  2  2  2  2
   3  4  5  6  7  8  9 10 11 12
      3  3  3  3  3  3  3  3  3
      4  5  6  7  8  9 10 11 12
         4  4  4  4  4  4  4  4
         5  6  7  8  9 10 11 12
            5  5  5  5  5  5  5
            6  7  8  9 10 11 12
               6  6  6  6  6  6
               7  8  9 10 11 12
                  7  7  7  7  7
                  8  9 10 11 12
                     8  8  8  8
                     9 10 11 12
                        9  9  9
                       10 11 12
                          10 10
                          11 12
                             11
                             12
```

Continue to use red ink for all your practice because in chapter eight you can see how we agree or disagree about what goes into the back yard garden (a common occurrence in many households).

Many individuals we've worked with have suggested that the sequence in which the objectives are presented will influence the outcome of the comparative valuation. We've tested this and found that the sequence has little or no measurable effect upon results.

You have probably noticed that as the number of objectives grows the time required and complexity expands considerably. Dr. Land told me that one multi-national corporation uses 44 objectives—but only after writing a computer program to tabulate data. The largest number of objectives we have personally used on a manual system was 23 and our preference is 20.

To assist you below is a table of check digits (number of circles) based upon the number of objectives used.

10 — 45
11 — 55
12 — 66
13 — 78
14 — 91
15 — 105
16 — 120
17 — 136
18 — 153
19 — 171
20 — 190

It is *most important* that this paired weighting be performed on an individual process only. Even if a group of people are in the same room working on a common problem, comparative valuation *must* be done individually. In chapter nine we will examine methods used in combining individual values into a useful group decision.

chapter seven
SATISFACTION IN THE NOW

A level of satisfaction is established on each option selected (as explained previously) to assist in determining the
amount of potential payback the user of this system might
expect. To illustrate this point let us say that two items (A &
B) have the same relative value but your level of satisfaction
(how happy you are today with what you've got) on Item A
is 90 per cent while on Item B you're only 35 per cent satisfied. Which offers the big payback? B of course. The incremental return on investment of your resources (time, money,
love, etc.) is potentially greater for Item B than for A. Another way to look at this is that A only has 10 per cent potential growth until you are 100 per cent satisfied while Item B
offers the opportunity for 65 per cent growth to reach the
total of 100 per cent level.

When developing the relative value of the selected objectives we compared each item to every other item—once. To

establish a level of satisfaction each item in the objective list is treated separately. The pair weighting or comparative valuation also deals with "future" wants. Remember the suggestion, "If I could have either A or B in equal amounts which would I like (future) just a little more of?" With level of satisfaction we must deal only in the *here and now*. It is impossible to guesstimate how satisfied we'll be next week or next year. Our level of satisfaction with any situation two weeks ago or five years ago has little meaning arriving at a decision *today*. Therefore use the question: "How satisfied am I with _____ today?"

The scale of satisfaction will range from 0 per cent to 100 per cent. Any percentage is acceptable so long as it is the individual true subjective judgment of *one* person at *one* point in time. It is most important not to attempt to use group process in determining satisfaction because the strongest group member will prevail.

If zero represents total dissatisfaction and 100 per cent means complete satisfaction, then 50 per cent is the midpoint which can be labeled "just getting by." The individual who ranks an item at 50 per cent is neither happy nor sad, neither too much nor too little, neither hot nor cold on that item. This 50 per cent line will represent one axis of the graph which we'll establish in the next chapter.

Don't allow yourself to get bogged down during this phase. Percentage satisfaction of 25 per cent, 40 per cent or 75 per cent is realistic. A number such as 23.926 per cent can only serve to delay the process and any subjective assessment to the third decimal might be considered suspect. Use even numbers in graduations of five or ten. As you will see later; being five of ten off will have little impact on the results.

When working on future oriented planning projects you may encounter objectives that, in the here and now, do not exist for you. If something does not exist in your experience or present situation you have only two choices for a level of satisfaction. Option one: You are totally dissatisfied with the fact that you do not have this item and would give it a big, fat *zero;* or Option two: you personally don't give a hoot one way or the other. You're getting by without it—as a matter of fact, "Who cares!" The per cent level to write down in this case is 50 per cent. You will never use over 50 per cent because it is impossible to be satisfied with something you don't have. An example might be space travel or a trip to the moon (if I was planning a vacation and trying to decide where to go). I'd put down 50 per cent because I couldn't care less. If I really had a strong desire to go and was unhappy with my inability to become an astronaut or my inability to book passage on the Columbia, I would write down a zero.

Enough discussion—let's try it. Below and in the study guide are the first examples of pair weighting with the author's personal levels of satisfaction (as of the date of this manuscript at 37,000 feet somewhere between Chicago and Tucson with a gin game going strong in the A & B seats—I think B seat will pay for her flight).

	VALUE			% SATISFACTION	
	MINE	YOURS		MINE	YOURS
1) Supervisor training	5			40	
2) Quality circles	5			50	
3) Cross training	7			30	
4) Piece work bonuses	4			55	
5) Flex time	7			35	
6) Four day week	4			30	
7) New equipment	1			50	
8) Air conditioning	7			20	
9) Employee health spa	0			0	
10) Child day care	5			65	

Before going on, write down *your* per cent levels of satisfaction in red on the blank spaces provided here or in the study guide. When putting your numbers in ignore the values the authors have placed on the objectives and our per cent levels of satisfaction; just evaluate "how satisfied *you* are" with each item (all by itself) at this point in time.

For those readers in a big hurry—go back and write in the percentages. Take the time to smell the daisies before they're growing out of your chest.

Your numbers are different than mine??? *Good!!!* This simply means that we're different people with different life experiences and we'll show you how we can join forces later on. For now notice that the per cent level of satisfaction numbers are *not* based upon value. Values show future and satisfaction is in the here and now. These are totally different measures—value always has a check digit (for ten the total is 45) *but* satisfaction can be anything from 0–100 and has no check digit.

Personal growth, corporate or organizational growth is based upon needs and wants. The energy for growth and change is often generated by discomfort, discontent or dissatisfaction.

You have participated in the painful process of change many times; now we can graphically display those areas of change representing the highest payback.

Fast trackers can move on now or utilize the practice below.

Opening up new methods can be exciting but the constant desire of the body and mind to seek homeostasis can be detrimental. The well worn path—practice makes perfect—these are comforting but restrictive slogans.

The examples from previous chapters are carried on below for purpose of practice. The per cent levels of satisfaction listed are those of the authors and included for purposes of example only. The printed numbers relate to the authors' experience at their primary place of employment and show satisfaction at the time this manuscript was prepared. We've included the questions used to elicit a here and now response for each objective. Keep in mind that we all have different experiences. For you in your situation it is *your* level of satisfaction that counts so (with your red pen) enter your per cent levels of satisfaction adjacent to the authors' in the example on page 58 or in the study guide:

Example #1—Employee health

Each of these 18 questions concentrated on a single objective—some of which are presently available and others which, while not presently available, would be nice to have. All of the "how satisfied am I" questions can easily deal with what's presently available. As they relate to what does not yet exist it is necessary to reframe the objectives into a here and now answerable question.

Let's use #18, Weight control clinic as an example. At Forest Hospital we don't have one. Therefore it was necessary to rephrase the question on a very personal note and estimate "how satisfied am I with my weight?" If either author was 5'6" and tipped the scales at 235 pounds we probably would have put down a different level of satisfaction.

Keep in mind the fact that these percentages are in the *here* and *now*. People like to argue (or discuss in a heated conversation) about how good or bad things are where they work. If you are male, age 58, a smoker, and work in an asbestos plant, I seriously doubt if you will be able to agree—in your level of satisfaction as it relates to employee health—with a 25 year old female RN working in a hospital cardiac care center. Expect differences in this *individual* decision process. We'll discuss getting together as a group later.

The purpose of these examples and really this whole

1)	Exercise program	How satisfied am I today with my exercise program?	30% _____
2)	Annual physicals	How satisfied am I with my health measurement program?	65% _____
3)	Employee assistance program	How satisfied am I with my company's EAP?	60% _____
4)	Health education program	How satisfied am I with my company's health education program?	50% _____
5)	Employee health spa	How satisfied am I with the availability of a spa?	50% _____
6)	Health goals	How satisfied am I with our goals program?	75% _____
7)	Stop smoking clinic	How satisfied am I with our stop smoking clinic?	0% _____
8)	Flex time	How satisfied am I with my present schedule?	80% _____
9)	Management commitment	How committed is upper management to improve health or how satisfied am I with their commitment?	85% _____
10)	Free meds	How satisfied am I with the cost of medication right now?	60% _____
11)	Exercise breaks	How satisfied am I with our scheduled exercise breaks?	25% _____
12)	Biofeedback	How satisfied am I with my knowledge of biofeedback and my access to it?	50% _____
13)	Health pay	How satisfied am I with extra pay for staying healthy?	50% _____
14)	Three week vacation	How satisfied am I with my present amount of paid vacation?	40% _____
15)	Accumulate sick days	How satisfied am I with our unused sick pay accumulation policy?	100% _____
16)	Relaxation breaks	How satisfied am I with opportunity to relax during my work day (coffee breaks)?	100% _____
17)	Shorter hours	How satisfied am I with the length of my work day?	100% _____
18)	Weight control clinic	How satisfied am I with my weight control program?	100% _____

book is to avoid wasting time in "meaningless" group discussions. After we get individual measurements on paper we can then discuss differences in a meaningful process designed to move ahead rather than in circles.

Let's try example #2. In this "veggie" example we can use two approaches. One can be from an organic gardener's point of view, the other will be from a consumer's point of view. The organic gardener might ask, "How satisfied am I with my ability to grow _____?" The consumer might ask, "How satisfied am I with the availability in my local store of fresh high quality _____?" I'm sure there are other viewpoints. The key is consistency—use *one* approach throughout any single process. If you'd like to look at a problem from several vantage points you need only change the question and go through the satisfaction process a second, third or fourth time—then compare the responses on the graph as shown in chapter eight.

Being organic gardeners we personally lean toward that approach but we'll use the consumer approach here because of its much broader based appeal to the general population.

The key question is, "How satisfied am I with the availability in my local store of nice, fresh, high quality _____?"

1) Peas	0	_____	7) Lettuce	10	_____
2) Parsley	30	_____	8) Garlic	100	_____
3) Cauliflower	75	_____	9) Carrots	80	_____
4) Cucumbers	50	_____	10) Tomatoes	20	_____
5) Dill	75	_____	11) Green Onions	60	_____
6) Squash	60	_____	12) Broccoli	60	_____

Again our levels of satisfaction will vary based upon experience, where we live (Anchorage vs Albuquerque) and what we use the vegetables for (i.e., one person might use cucumbers to make dill pickles so he would need them by the bushel; another uses them in salads and needs them one at a time).

Now that we covered how to get value and satisfaction numbers for each objective, let's move on to what to do with all the numbers we've got.

chapter eight
PLOTTING AND INTERPRETING THE PROFILE

To simplify the analysis of the numbers (values and levels of satisfaction) generated in the previous chapters we can now plot each objective on a graphic display. The graph which will prove most effective is a simple piece of one-fourth inch graph paper. The study guide has all of the charts used in this chapter. If one of these is not available you can draw a few simple lines on any piece of paper. (Many a decision has been graphically shown on a cocktail napkin.)

The graph shown in the fast track and supplemental examples are for the authors' numbers. We encourage you to plot your numbers (again in red ink) directly on the applicable chart in the study guide or below.

The design of the graph is quite simple. The vertical axis is used to represent the values established in the pair weighting exercise. The length of the vertical axis is determined by the number of objectives chosen. The productivity example consisted of 10 objectives. Therefore the vertical axis looks like:

```
9
8
7
6
5
4
3
2
1
0
```

Merely listing the objectives by their value will give you a rank order of importance list. Fun to look at but still an unidimensional measure. From a rank order or highest to lowest list we cannot determine which objective will provide maximum potential payback. This payback can be identified using the second measurement which we called—per cent level of satisfaction. The per cent satisfaction numbers are shown on a horizontal axis going from zero (0) to 100 per cent with the 50 per cent point being just getting by. The satisfaction line will look like:

| 100 | 90 | 80 | 70 | 60 | 50 | 40 | 30 | 20 | 10 | 0 |

When combining the two (V and per cent) you will notice that the vertical (value) axis always crosses the horizontal (satisfaction) axis at the 50 per cent point. The horizontal axis will cross the vertical axis at the halfway point. (This is determined by the number of objectives selected.) In the fast track example we chose 10 objectives so the horizontal axis will intersect the vertical at the value of 5.

To develop a pictorial view for analysis we now plot each objective in its appropriate place. The productivity example revealed the following:

(We've left space for you on the following page and in the

```
                              9
                              8
                              7
                              6
 100  90  80  70  60        5    40  30  20  10  0
                              4
                              3
                              2
                              1
                              0
```

		Authors' Numbers		Readers' Numbers	
Ref #	Objective	Value	% S	Value	% S
1)	Supervisior training	5	40		
2)	Quality circles	5	50		
3)	Cross training	7	30		
4)	Piece work bonus	4	55		
5)	Flex time	7	35		
6)	Four day week	4	30		
7)	New equipment	1	50		
8)	Air conditioning	7	20		
9)	Employee health spa	0	0		
10)	Child day care	5	65		

study guide to bring your numbers forward for purposes of comparison.) Starting with Supervisors training (Objective #1) take the value (5) and move up the value axis until you reach that value. Then take the per cent satisfaction and move right or left until you are in line with the appropriate per cent on the horizontal axis. At this point you write in the objective reference number as shown in the example on the following page. Draw a circle around the reference number to distinguish it from the background graph numbers.

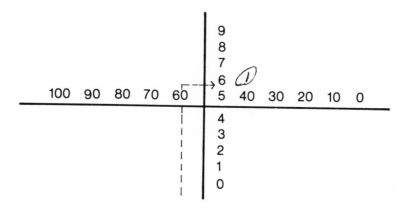

Continue this process with each of the objectives until you have them all plotted on the graph which when completed will look like this:

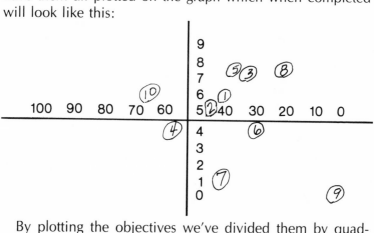

By plotting the objectives we've divided them by quadrant. Each quadrant has a different significance and there are some gray "borderline" areas. Let's start with the upper left quadrant. Into this area will fall those items with a relatively high value (we care about them significantly) and those items having above a 50 per cent level of current satisfaction. (We are also fairly pleased with how much of these items we presently have.) These can be called givens or what we've already got as it relates to the selected objectives. Because of the currently high level of satisfaction we can not expect significant improvement or high additional payback by investing greater energies here. These items should be maintained because of their value.

It is in the "given" classification that we find a significant departure from the nice "straight" lines of the graph. High value/high satisfaction items in most situations include mid-range (value and satisfaction) items which are necessary just to keep the ship afloat or the business running. In this technique they show up as a lobe extending one or two points below the satisfaction axis and for about 5 per cent on either side of the value axis.

In the productivity example the givens include the objectives: 2—quality circles, 4—piecework bonuses, and 10—child day care. If we were to draw a line around the given area it would look like:

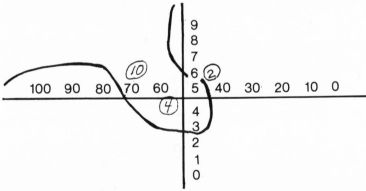

The second area to consider is the lower left quadrant. The objectives which plot in this area are those of relatively low value with high satisfaction. These are items which don't mean that much to us but we've got a lot of them. This *"too much"* area can be called overkill. Why do objectives fall in here? Why do we waste time on these? The answer lies in the fact that most individuals and all organizations do certain things very well—they have always done these things well—

they don't know why. They have never evaluated payback and the best answer is probably "because." In this overkill area you might find resources which could be better allocated for higher payback.

The lower right hand quadrant represents the third area. In this sector you'll find items of low value and low satisfaction. If you were to interview people—one on one—about their needs you often get complaints. These are very safe to talk about because no one really cares and nothing will be done beyond talk. This area contains the *don't wants* or *gripes.*

In group problem solving sessions these low value/low satisfaction items are terrific time wasters and can be most effectively used to avoid making any decision. By using this decision making model you can quickly identify what is not important. Now you can direct energies to more fruitful areas such as those found in:

The upper right area of the graph. In this fourth quadrant will be found those items of relatively *high value* but *low* levels of *current satisfaction.* These items provide the greatest opportunity for growth and payback. These are the true wants regarding any situation. By drawing low or no payback resources from the overkill/gripe areas and investing them in the high payback *wants* or opportunity area you will maximize your return on available investment.

By looking at the total *productivity* picture we can answer our initial question: How can I improve productivity here at XYZ manufacturing?

The question has been answered and the decision of one person has been made (we'll carry this example through the group process in later chapters) regarding which objectives offer the highest potential payback and point directly at *how to* get the job done.

Looking at the graphic picture on the following page, we now can see that objectives #2 (quality circles), 4 (piece work bonuses) and 10 (child day care) should be maintained

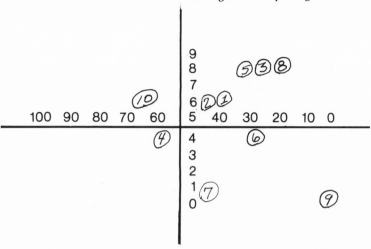

at their present levels—no further investment is justified at this point.

Objectives numbered 6 (four day week), 7 (new equipment) and 9 (employee health spa) will be fun to talk about but have very minimal worth. It is usually at this point in the process that an individual will say, "Hold it! The numbers are wrong! This is not the way I feel! I've been tricked! I think a four day week and a health spa are very important— they're not gripes!" Since the process is so time efficient, the answer to this phenomenon of disbelief is to redo the paired weighting and current satisfaction process. Use the same objectives in the same reference number order, or change the sequence; it won't matter. Then reevaluate for value and per cent. When the objectives fall in the same relative graphic placement, you'll see that perhaps you're trying to tell yourself something. (On several occasions the authors have personally redone the evaluation three or four times before they individually decided not to attempt to rationalize away the truth.)

The areas of high payback include 1 (supervisor training), 3 (cross training), 5 (flex time) and 8 (air conditioning) with #8 being the strongest.

Take a moment to plot in and evaluate your red ink values and percentages to see how we agree or disagree.

We'll continue with this example in chapter ten where we will look at the results of the entire XYZ management team with which a plan of action can be implemented.

Example #1—Employee health

To display graphically the Employee health example we need to construct a graph for 18 objectives. Using the same methods used earlier we assign value to the vertical axis and use the horizontal axis for level of current satisfaction. The value (vertical) axis will intersect the horizontal at the 50 per cent point but since the number of objectives has changed—so has the vertical point of intersection. The horizontal always intersects the vertical at the midpoint. Since we are using 18 objectives the intersection will be across the number 9 as shown below. (Note: the maximum possible value is always one less than the number of objectives; therefore the horizontal axis goes through halfway.) We've brought the values from chapters six and seven forward to work with and there's a place for you to bring your numbers along on the following page.

To plot objective #1 move up the value axis to the appropriate value (11 in this case) and then move left or right to the appropriate per cent level of satisfaction, which for Exercise programs would be 30 per cent. Write the objective reference number (found in the far left hand column) at the point where Value 11 and 30 per cent intersect. Circle the number. To plot objective #2 (annual physicals) move up the value axis to 4 and left to the 65 per cent line—write in the #2 and circle it.

Continue this process until all 18 objective reference numbers have been plotted to their respective coordinates. The decision making profile for Employee health is on page 70.

Ref #	Objective	Authors' Numbers		Readers' Numbers	
		Value	%	Value	%
1	Exercise programs	11	30		
2	Annual physicals	4	65		
3	Employee assistance	9	60		
4	Health education	14	50		
5	Employee health spa	9	50		
6	Health goals (MBO's)	14	75		
7	Stop smoking clinic	10	0		
8	Flexible time	10	80		
9	Management commitment	15	85		
10	Free medication	0	60		
11	Exercise breaks	9	25		
12	Biofeedback	4	50		
13	Health pay	2	50		
14	Three week vacation	15	40		
15	Accumulated sick pay	4	100		
16	Relaxation breaks	13	100		
17	Shorter hours	1	100		
18	Weight control clinic	9	80		

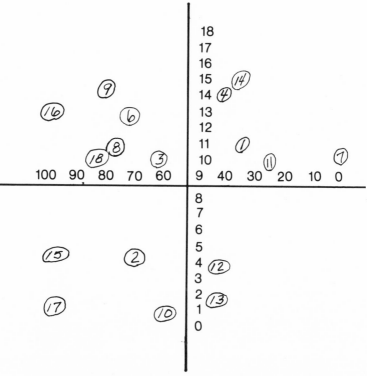

Take a moment to plot your red Employee health numbers on this same graph.

In analyzing the black numbers we would classify numbers:

3 Employee assistance program
5 Employee health spa
6 Health goals (MBOs)
8 Flexable time
9 Management commitment
16 Relaxation breaks
18 Weight control clinic

as givens (high value/high satisfaction) to the individual doing this evaluation (One author). Numbers:

2 Annual physicals
10 Free medication
15 Accumulated sick days
17 Shorter hours

are nice clean overkills (got too much); while the objectives with reference number 12—Biofeedback and 13—Health pay are low value gripes—personally, and these are one author's personal numbers; he couldn't care less about these two.

The opportunities for big payback include what I *want:*

Ref no.	Objectives
1	Exercise programs
4	Health education
7	Stop smoking clinic
11	Exercise breaks
14	Three weeks vacation

Now analyze your personal profile. Transfer your objective reference numbers to one of the categories below or in the study guide:

GIVENS (Upper Left)	OVERKILL (Lower Left)	GRIPES (Lower Right)	WANTS (Upper Right)

Transfer resources from your overkills and gripes to the want area and you can expect high incremental payback. Be sure to maintain the givens.

Example #2—Veggies

The process seems to work quite well for big decisions regarding Productivity and Health—will it work on a Saturday afternoon in the back yard with organic soil under your fingernails?

Using the same process the authors have developed the following graphic display of a vegetable garden. There is ample room below to bring your red numbers along from chapters six and seven.

Ref no.	Objective	Authors' Numbers		Readers' Numbers	
		Value	%	Value	%
1	Peas	9	0		
2	Parsley	6	30		
3	Cauliflower	2	75		
4	Cucumbers	8	50		
5	Dill	1	75		
6	Squash	7	60		
7	Lettuce	9	10		
8	Garlic	0	100		
9	Carrots	3	80		
10	Tomatoes	11	20		
11	Green Onions	6	40		
12	Broccoli	4	60		

Analyzing this profile (from a Veggie consumer standpoint) we quickly see that the author should continue to grow #6—squash—his only given. We will not waste time buying seed for:

    3 Cauliflower
    5 Dill
    8 Garlic
    9 Carrots
   12 Broccoli

because they are low value with poor payback. We seem to have two groupings of opportunities. The strongest *wants* are 1—peas, 7—lettuce, and 10—tomatoes to which we will give ample space. The second group of wants include 2—parsley, 5—cucumbers and 11—green onions with which we'll round out the garden. Trying to plant too many things in a garden is similar to trying to do too many projects at once at the office—anything can go to seed, wither and die if not properly cared for.

chapter nine
FROM INDIVIDUAL TO GROUP

Up to this point we have concentrated on the process of decision-making as it relates to the individual. By working through the process you have creatively examined all of your options, picked the most likely, established a value and level of current satisfaction, and objectively determined the highest payback options or opportunities for solving a problem or making a decision.

This is all well and good, but in real life few of us operate in a vacuum. In most situations; at work, in community groups or at home we operate as part of a group.

This group interaction exerts a very strong influence upon what we do in the area of making decisions and solving problems. Often an individual can put forward an excellent solution to a problem yet find the group non-receptive or even antagonistic. An individual operating on his own can make decisions, short and long term, which affect only his future with relative impunity. The problem arises when the decision of one person affects other group members. This is often the reason why a person can enjoy great entrepreneurial success in running a one man corporation or business. But, when the company grows and additional employees are added with layers of management (President, Vice President, Managers and Supervisors) the thriving concern up to this point develops management and structure problems. The basis of these problems often arises from the often used cliche, "There seems to be a failure to communicate."

The decision maker is always willing to let others know the decision—but he is often unwilling, or, more importantly, unable to share the reasons behind the solution or the steps leading up to the decision. This worked fine in less enlightening times when participatory management was not yet the norm. In today's world of involvement (i.e., unions, women's rights, quality circles, equal employment opportunities) there is a definable need for a decision-making process in which all members of a group can take part. The process must be time efficient and broadly applicable to many widely varied situations.

In group problem-solving the decision maker (as an individual) often finds a group unreceptive or antagonistic. It is no wonder that individuals "pull in their horns" and "go with the flow" when joining a new group. If every time I suggest a solution (make a decision on my own) my coworkers change the subject and give me 75 reasons why my solution won't work—you can bet your bottom dollar I'll evaluate and reevaluate every thought I have before I open my mouth. This atmosphere generates and encourages the functional fixation discussed in chapter two.

The opposite also occurs. A very bad decision made by the strongest group member, group leader, company president or committee chairman is often jammed down the group members' throats. They acquiesce because they have no efficient, non-conflictual method with which to find the best group solution.

Several years ago a major corporation was planning a territory division between two regional offices of a distribution company. The territory in question was the state of Montana. The primary population centers of Montana are in the western one third of the state which was only 850 miles from region office B. The territory belonged to region office A which was 1200 miles away. The market area remained in A because the A region manager had more political power than either the B region manager or the National Director of Distribution. In spite of "logical evidence" in favor of the territory change agreed to by most people involved, the "final" decision hinged upon the power of one politically savvy region manager. If the corporation had used a participatory versus an advisory decision-making system the results would, quite probably, have been different. Incidentally, when the manager of region A was promoted to a national position a few years later he "saw the light" and supported the transfer.

To solve these two major group problems we need a procedure which can satisfy both extremes not only separately but often in the same group. The procedure must encourage participation yet provide a clear direction to all involved; recognize experience yet also not discount new arrivals—be they people—equipment—techniques—or ideas.

The Creative Decision-Making process does fulfill all these requirements, plus it provides a picture for all to see.

Since we're discussing pictures, this is a good spot to discuss the preferred layout of the room. Through years of practice we've found the ideal layout to be a flat bottomed "V" with the open end fairly near a blank wall.

The flat "V" can be easily expanded to accommodate any workable size group plus each participant can see what's going on at all times. Be sure to provide elbow room for comfort while working the pair weighting sheets and graphs.

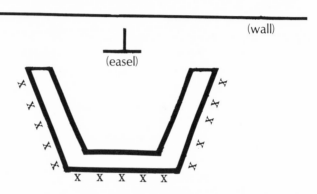

An easel with a large pad of paper provides the group facilitator a convenient method for recording ideas. The blank wall is a great place to display all the ideas generated. (Use masking tape which is easy to remove—*never* use scotch tape!)

After reading this book you probably are ready to serve as a group facilitator. To clearly understand applicability to group process let's review the five steps with an eye toward the group. In reviewing the steps:

Step #1—The purge, divergent thought or idea generating phase (perhaps the most important) can be done individually or in group. Again we must stress that in this step the group generates ideas—not good ideas—just lots of ideas. The secretary writes each idea on the easel pad in large print so everyone can read it. Each group member is encouraged to verbally purge or state out loud the idea as it is generated. One person's idea will often trigger another participant who will blurt out another idea—every idea is recorded by the facilitator. By writing each idea—no matter how silly, disjointed or absurd—we reinforce and recognize the participant which, in turn, encourages other people to volunteer, get involved, take risks and speak up.

The encouragement is *not* verbal! The response given to an idea is only written. It is important that the secretary maintain a neutral stance. The secretary must not use such terms as: *great, good, fine, good idea,* etc. By using such encouraging words, the participants will be getting the message that they should generate only *"good"* ideas which will overlay evaluation on the process thus defeating the purpose of the purge and inhibit pure idea generation. As each sheet of easel pad paper is filled up the secretary tears it off and tapes it up on the wall for all to see.

We've found the ideal group size to be between 8 and 15. Any group larger than 16 or so gets cumbersome. (Once, using this process we facilitated a group of 42—never again!) The group must have a common interest in the problem and they must feel that the results of their efforts will at least have a chance of being implemented. Nothing stifles creativity faster than knowing beforehand that the effort will be an exercise in futility. Use the same fixation breaking techniques for groups as you would if you were doing this as an individual.

Step #2—As with idea generation the convergent thought or objective setting phase works very well in a group. The reason for success is the elimination of evaluation from these two phases. All group members review the ideas taped up on the wall to select their best shots. Any members of the group can speak up and volunteer an idea without ridicule and the secretary writes the idea down in large print on the easel pad. In earlier chapters we worked with 10, 12, and 18 objectives in an individual process. When a *group* selects objectives we've found the number chosen usually leans toward the 15 to 20 range. This is good because it allows every member to get his "favorite" onto the objective list and encourages continued participation. A rule of thumb says: have at least as many objectives as group members before you begin pair weighting. Another point to remember in group is to clearly define what is meant by each objective so that there is a common base of knowledge. (i.e., If I wrote down EAP on the objective sheet those members not familiar with industrial alcoholism treatment would not only now know what EAP was, they would also not know what an Employee Assistance Program was supposed to do.) When all the objectives are listed next to their reference numbers the objectives sheet is taped up on the wall.

Step #3—The comparative valuation (paired weighting) phase is *always* done individually. The reason for this is to get at the true feelings of each individual group member. Each participant uses a separate work sheet and the *same* reference number order of the objectives. This is a must if we are to accurately develop a total group graphic display. When facilitating this valuation process we will read the choices aloud so that each group member can concentrate on answering the, "If I could have 1—peas or 12—broccoli which would I like a little more of?" The facilitator reading the list must take special care not to prejudice the group by using influential statements or voice inflection, i.e., "If I could have 1—peas or 12—*broccoli!. . . .*" This can happen unintentionally especially if the person reading this list is the boss of the people doing the paired weighting.

A couple of years ago the vice president of a large insurance company called to say the managers of his division tried the program and supported *exactly* his ideas of how to solve a particular problem. We asked who ran the group. He stated that he did. We suggested that since he gave them their raises, hired, fired and promoted them, his presence might be heavily influential. The next week he went on vacation leaving instructions that the group use the process again on the same problem. When he returned he received a group profile that was in no way similar to the first.

The group had found some new and creative options and presented the vice president with what they felt would be the best solution to the problem. The best decision was made using the Creative Decision-Making model plus a good management practice called delegation. Even though the vice president was a well liked, fair and intelligent person—in this situation his very presence (plus being the facilitator) biased the results. A similar experience occurred when conducting a program for a major association; the group working on the problem was extremely reserved—almost uptight. At the coffee break the vice president of marketing introduced me to the chairman of the board—*ouch!* This man was so powerful he stifled almost every person in the room. After explaining the situation to the chairman he was gracious enough to take an early lunch. Upon getting together after coffee the entire group operated with total freedom of speech. To take advantage of this *new energy* we went back to step one and started the purge all over again. The group needed little encouragement, having already experienced the process earlier that morning. We developed a group profile one half hour earlier than expected.

When you are working with this or any process in a group setting and things don't feel right—find out as soon as possible what the group's immediate problem is so you can move forward. A group with lockjaw will go "nowhere fast!"

Step #4—As with Step #3, the current satisfaction estimation process is a 100 per cent individual activity for the same reasons mentioned for Step #3. Each participant writes down on their worksheet the per cent level of satisfaction with each objective.

Step #5—Plotting the profile for a group is done in exactly the same way as for an individual with one intervening step, finding the group average value and per cent satisfaction for each objective. This can be done quite quickly (for a group of 15 we've done the calculations in less than one hour while the group was at lunch). The process is simple mechanics. After every group participant has written down their per cent level of current satisfaction ask them to write their names on their worksheets (the one containing both the value and per cent satisfaction). Collect all the sheets and average the numbers. We use a group worksheet like the one below (also found in your study guide).

Participant	A	B	C	D				Total	Avg.
1									
2									
3									
4									

Any sheet of lined accounting paper will do or you can make your own. After collecting the worksheets each is assigned an alpha code (A, B, C, D, etc.). Then on one group worksheet (as above) we transcribe each individual's values which correspond to his objective reference numbers. On a separate group worksheet we transcribe each participant's level of current satisfaction. We go through the trouble to transcribe so we can return the participant's sheets to them and still retain the detail. Next total each line—simply add from left to right and divide this total by the number of participants to get the average. On the following pages are the worksheets for the productivity example. We've selected 10 participants because the battery in our calculator is dead and 10 is an easy number to divide by. (In real life neither author has ever worked with a nice even 10).

These two worksheets give us all the detail necessary to plot and interpret a group profile.

Several years ago Dr. Randall Thompson, President of the Forest Institute of Professional Psychology, worked with us in conducting a session with 35 participants who came up with 31 objectives. The size of the group and the volume of the data required a computer programmed not only to give us averages; but since we had access to the machine, we had it print out mean, median and standard deviation. It was a great deal of fun but we find the simple worksheets with smaller groups to be as effective in developing a meaningful graphic display of high payback objectives. Keep in mind that is the decision we're after—not the glory of the process. When looking at the "average" column you'll immediately notice we no longer have nice clean whole numbers for values and the per cent levels of satisfaction are no longer round numbers. This can make exact placement of the objectives more difficult. Do not concern yourself with their precise placement because it is the relative placement which will determine which objectives are the groups high payback opportunities.

With a small number of objectives such as the ten used in the productivity example we can again plot out the graphic picture on simple graph paper. As the number of objectives gets larger (say 18 or 20), or if the group working on the problem is large (12–25) you might consider using an expanded graph. With an individual profile one graph square (¼ inch) could represent a change of value of one or a change in per cent level of satisfaction to 10 illustrated on the individual graph. When plotting averages we often use

PRODUCTIVITY VALUE WORKSHEET

Obj. # s

Participant	A	B	C	D	E	F	G	H	I	J	Total	Avg.
1	5	7	4	6	8	3	5	7	6	7	58	5.8
2	5	5	7	8	4	5	6	6	7	6	59	5.9
3	7	4	5	8	7	6	7	5	9	8	66	6.6
4	4	5	7	5	6	3	7	5	4	5	52	5.2
5	7	4	6	5	7	6	8	4	7	5	56	5.6
6	4	6	5	7	5	5	8	6	4	5	55	5.5
7	1	3	1	0	2	4	1	3	2	1	18	1.8
8	7	5	1	2	1	4	2	5	3	4	34	3.4
9	0	2	3	1	3	2	0	4	2	0	17	1.7
10	5	4	6	3	2	7	1	0	1	4	33	3.3

PRODUCTIVITY PER CENT SATISFACTION WORKSHEET

Participant	A	B	C	D	E	F	G	H	I	J	Total	Avg.
1	40	60	50	75	75	55	70	80	60	75	640	64
2	50	50	70	60	40	50	30	100	90	70	610	61
3	30	40	10	0	25	30	40	60	15	40	290	29
4	55	75	60	90	65	40	75	100	50	60	670	67
5	35	30	50	10	50	50	25	50	40	30	370	37
6	30	40	60	10	50	35	0	50	0	15	290	29
7	50	75	95	100	85	50	75	100	80	90	800	80
8	20	10	40	50	35	15	25	50	40	20	305	30
9	0	50	50	0	50	0	50	0	0	50	250	25
10	65	75	100	40	100	100	50	100	50	75	755	75

Obj.#s

100	90	80	70	60	5'	40	30	20	10	0
					10					
					9					
					8					
					7					
					6					
					4					
					3					
					2					
					1					

INDIVIDUAL

four squares to represent one value or 10 per cent as shown on the following page.

The expanded scale also works well with groups because of the natural tendancy for group averages to be just that—averages. While individual members of any group may have extreme high or low values the group as a whole will move toward the middle. After the mechanical process of developing group concensus (in which each and every member took part) those objectives which fall into the upper right quadrant have not only high payback potential but also a very good chance of being implemented and followed up on. This is

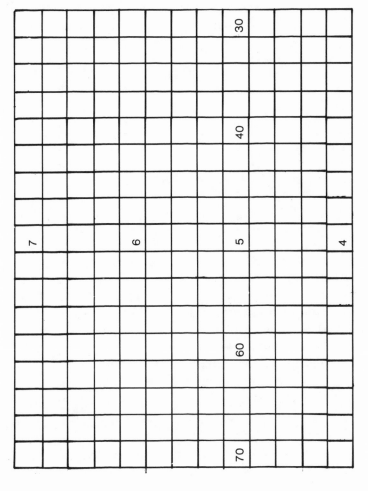

GROUP

because the group agrees and will work as a whole toward these objectives.

The process of plotting the group numbers is exactly the same as that for individuals.

PRODUCTIVITY OBJECTIVES	AUTHORS #'s		GROUP #'s		YOUR NUMBERS	
Ref # OBJECTIVE	VALUE	%	VALUE	%	VALUE	%
1 Supervisor training	5	40	5.8	61	_____	_____
2 Quality circles	5	50	5.9	61	_____	_____
3 Cross training	7	30	6.6	29	_____	_____
4 Piece work bonus	4	55	5.2	67	_____	_____
5 Flex time	7	35	5.6	37	_____	_____
6 Four day week	4	30	5.5	29	_____	_____
7 New equipment	1	50	1.8	80	_____	_____
8 Air conditioning	7	20	3.4	30	_____	_____
9 SPA	0	0	1.7	25	_____	_____
10 Day care	5	65	3.3	75	_____	_____

The group profile is on page 89.

Notice that we drew small squares around the group numbers. The reason for doing this is to distinguish them from the individual profile carried forward from chapter eight. In any group process there is room for difference of opinion and by plotting your individual profile in red on the same sheet of graph paper with the group profile and the author's numbers you will find areas of agreement. Also, and equally as important, you will often find differences. These differences should be addressed with questions such as:

*Do I know something about the situation that the rest of the group doesn't know?

*Does the group know something I'm not aware of?

By answering these types of questions there will be an automatic sharing of information which should benefit the group as a whole as well as the individual. It is also an excellent

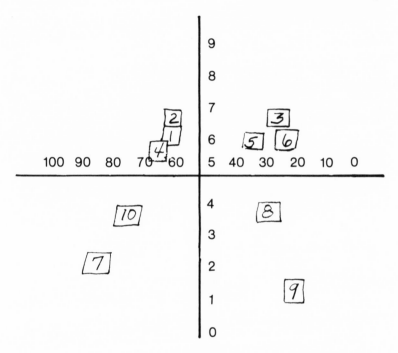

way to highlight why your pet project has been successful or a flop. The successful project will show high group agreement and support. Your personal unsuccessful projects will plot out in a quadrant other than the group norm.

Let us look again at the profile but this time we'll show a composite of the authors', the group's and yours as illustrated on the following page.

Analyzing the agreements and disagreements between the authors' and group's profiles we find that in the opportunity zone we have agreement on the objectives 3 and 5. The agreement here means all will support 3—Cross training and a move toward 5—Flex time. The objective 6—Four day week is also fairly close and since it is very similar to 5—Flex time in meaning we could combine the two concepts and work out a solution.

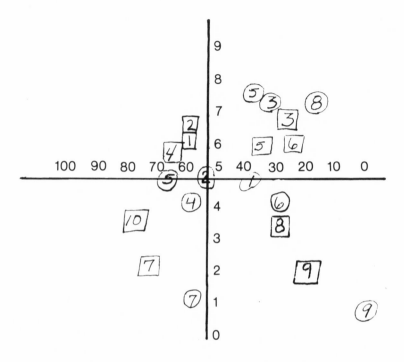

Now look at those items in the opportunity quadrant which show up only once—either in a square or circle. Start with 8—Air conditioning—"Good grief my strongest opportunity—but the whole group sees it as a gripe. Are they totally insensitive to my needs—what kind of penny pinching low life would expect me to cook while they're all cool as cucumbers!" *Stop!* What has just happened in the Air conditioning example is something called blame. Blame and accusation never solve any problems so let's start over.

"My strongest opportunity is #8 and the group sees it as a gripe. *Is there something they know that I don't?* A bit of research might show that the production area and every other office is cool except mine. I've been suffering in silence. (I've always been the grin and bear it type.) My air conditioning problems are not affecting productivity elsewhere in the company and this group process exercise is directed at productivity. How about my productivity? Air conditioning affects it directly—my personal problem. I'll solve that problem with a single call to the maintenance department. While awaiting repairs I'll remove my jacket, vest and tie to allow for maximum comfort under the unique circumstances." Now we can continue to analyze the profile.

The authors have numbers 1—Supervisor training and 2—Quality circles in the upper right but the group sees them as givens. Perhaps we've been putting more emphasis on these areas than they warrant. The group seems to be quite satisfied with our levels in these two areas so let's maintain an ongoing program with continued management support but make no major investment here.

The differences have been resolved and the solution to the productivity problem seems to lie in the areas of 3—Cross training and 5—Flex time or 6—a Four day week. We, as a group, have made a decision to explore these two areas and implement programs of improvement.

Programs of improvement almost always demand resource allocation decisions. Where will the resources come from to improve Training and Time. These might be found by looking at the global picture which is nicely presented on the graph.

First look at the overkill area. Are we placing too much emphasis on Day care? If we implement a four day week or flex time will we still need all or part of our day care program? Also in the overkill area is new equipment. Is it possible we're knee deep in the latest equipment with more on order? Now we know that this is not the total answer. We might even consider cancelling the recently placed order for the "left handed whatzit." This cancellation will free up dollars and space which might be used for a training department.

How about the gripe zone. Smith—the vice president of human resources planning has had an intern studying an employee health spa for the last nine weeks. Perhaps that intern could be switched over to study the health and productivity benefit potential of change in working hours? Or the intern could start developing a cross training schedule.

Once the high payback areas are identified it is possible to move very quickly to implement programs which will cash in on the opportunities. The total graphic picture often provides the resources.

The power of a group has been mentioned several times but it deserves additional comment. Management teams utilizing this process will enhance their joint ability to pull together while encouraging the individual members to evaluate their personal methods of measurement and/or feelings about any single area of interest. The process is non-threatening and provides a picture of how the individual and group view the future. By setting direction for the future a management team can more easily control their business. Volunteer groups such as the Cub Scout pack committee or the Church Men's Club can greatly benefit from Creative Decision-Making because these civic service or fraternal organizations have a charter but no formal plan of action. From an evaluation of objectives and the plotting of a profile "almost" any group can set direction and formulate a plan of action. Often the greatest problem area for volunteer groups (as well as more formal organizations) is that they have too many opportunities—choose too many and dilute their resources.

This dispersal of strength or dilution of resources can affect business as well as volunteer groups or a person's family. We encourage you to try the process with your family regarding the site for your family vacation.

After the high payback areas are pinpointed, the plan of

action should consider several items influencing the "after decision" implementation process. The decision maker's, individual or group, position in the management team will require different actions as determined by that position. These will be addressed in the next chapter.

chapter ten
THE NEXT STEP

Using the opportunities as a basis for future planning the individual or group can benefit from using a what, when, where, who, how often, how much and why approach.

WHAT: The opportunity profile has graphically displayed *what* the high payback areas consist of. By refining these objectives, combining them and rearranging them you'll very quickly be able to determine exactly what you wish to do.

WHEN: Ask the question, "Is timing of crucial importance or can these opportunities be integrated into day to day life?" The answer will shape your action plan as well as your calender.

WHERE: Where can refer to the exact location for opportunity implementation such as geographic location, specific building on campus or in which department a pilot program should be implemented.

WHO: Who will be affected by changes associated with

the implementation of new programs? Who might feel threatened by discontinuance of existing programs? Who will be involved? Who will be responsible? Who will have or presently has authority to OK investments? (The golden rule applies here—"The man with the gold makes the rules.") If the decision-making process was engaged in by a hospital board, a corporation executive committee or other such "final decision-making and authoritive group there will be minimal problem with this *who* question.

On the other hand if the oportunities were arrived at by a committee of supervisors they will need to identify exactly *who* has the authority to approve their recommendations. At this point the individual or group may benefit from a bit of research in "*how* to sell an idea." This can be done by listing the key opportunity (from the decision-making process) plus three or more alternate courses of action. After each potential action, list estimated costs and estimated returns. A chart such as the one below and in the study guide could prove useful:

Potential Action	Cost	Benefit
1 Key Opportunity	$, people, resources, etc.	$, PR, Morale, Productivity
2 Alternate		
3 Alternate		
4 Alternate		
5 Alternate		

For each potential action make a list, like the one on the following page, of potential objections the key decision maker might raise. Also list three ways each objection can be overcome.

Anyone who has taken an insurance sales course will recognize this method—anticipate objections and be ready for them. This, at first glance, might appear to be a great deal

Potential Objection	How to Overcome
1.	A B C
2.	A B C
3.	A B C

of work. It is key to selling your idea and taking advantage of the opportunities you've pinpointed. Be sure to load your gun before you go hunting—only you will know if the game you're after is a hummingbird or a *cape buffalo*—which will assist you in making the decision concerning the size of your gun. We've devoted considerable space to the *who* because of the key persons' impact upon *how often, how much* and *why* you're searching for improvement in the first place.

After approval and funding are received the task of implementation will be relatively easy. After implementation of change—directed and controlled change—the decision-making process can be used periodically ro refine or redirect the project. It can be a very frustrating experience to see a potentially high payback project fail because of lack of ongoing support. This decrease of support can be caused by any number of occurrences such as changing economic conditions, employee or staff changes of key management position changes to name a few. Based upon the size and complexity of your organization and the level of your involvement you might consider a half day planning session on a quarterly, semi-annual or annual basis. Into these sessions you can integrate any new team members (remember Purge and Set Objectives without evaluation). Mention must also be made that by using the decision-making process regularly you may find that because of changes you will need to make some difficult decisions concerning favorite projects which no longer offer high payback potential.

Several individuals we have worked with have found the process an excellent vehicle for the development of management reports. From buying a car to locating a new corporate office site this process offers flexibility—feel free to use any of the forms, charts or graphs in this text or in the study guide for your personal use. As far as we are concerned there will never be a copyright on the creative mind.

SUGGESTED READINGS

Below is a brief listing of some of the books touching on the subject of creativity, problem solving and decision making. When reading these, or any self-study book, we suggest you not read from cover to cover. You might benefit most by setting up a self education reading schedule — i.e. read 20 minutes or one chapter per day. This more leisurely approach allows time to fully digest and implement the knowledge gained. Good Luck!

Andrews, M., ed., *Creativity and Psychological Health*. Syracuse, NY: Syracuse, U., 1961.

Baker, S., *Your.Key to Creative Thinking*. New York: Bantam, 1964.

Barron, F., *Creative Person and Creative Process*. New York: Holt, 1969.

Biondi, A., ed., *The Creative Process.* Buffalo: D.O.K., 1973.

Bois, J., *The Art of Awareness* (2nd ed.) Dubuque, IA: W. C. Brown, 1973.

Bruner, J., *Beyond the Information Given.* New York: Norton, 1973.

Crawford, R., *The Techniques of Creative Thinking.* Wells, VT: Fraser, 1964.

Davis, G., *Psychology of Problem Solving.* New York: Basic Books, 1973.

De Bono, E., *Children Solve Problems.* New York: Harper and Row, 1972.

Ekvall, G., *Creativity at the Place of Work.* Stockholm: Swedish Council for Personnel Administration, 1971.

Fine, B., *Stretching Their Minds.* New York: Dutton, 1964.

Forem, J., *Transcendental Meditation.* New York: Dutton, 1974.

Fuller, R., *Operating Manual for Spaceship Earth.* Carbondale: Southern Illinois University, 1969.

Fuller, R. B., *Intuition.* Garden City, NY: Doubleday, 1972.

Garfield, P., *Creative Dreaming.* New York: Simon and Schuster, 1974.

Gowan, J., *Development of the Creative Individual.* San Diego: Knapp, 1972.

Guilford, J., *Intelligence, Creativity, and Their Educational Implications.* San Diego: Knapp, 1968.

Illich, I., *Deschooling Society.* New York: Harper and Row, 1971.

Karagulla, S., *Breakthrough to Creativity.* Los Angeles: De Vorss, 1967.

Land, G. L., *Grow or Die: The Principle of Transformation.* New York: Random House, 1973.

Maier, N., *Creative Management.* New York: Wiley, 1962.

Maslow, A. H., *The Farther Reaches of Human Nature.* New York: Viking/Esalen, 1972.

Mason, J. G., *How to Be a More Creative Executive.* New York: McGraw-Hill, 1960.

Neill, A., *Freedom — Not License!* New York: Hart, 1972.

Newell, A., and Simon, H. *Human Problem Solving.* Englewood Cliffs, NJ: Prentice-Hall, 1972.

Otto, H., *Group Methods to Actualize Human Potential: A Handbook.* Beverly Hills, CA: Holistic Press, 1970.

Parnes, S., *Creativity: Unlocking Human Potential.* Buffalo: D.O.K., 1972.

Parnes, S., Noller, R., and Hiondi, A., *Guide to Creative Action.* New York: Scribners, 1976.

Perls, F., *Gestalt Therapy Verbatim*. Lafayette, CA: Real People Press, 1969.

Piaget, J., Inhilder, B., et al., *Mental Imagery in the Child*. New York: Basic Books, 1971.

Rogers, C., *Carl Rogers on Encounter Groups*. New York: Harper and Row, 1970.

Schneider, L., *Be Careful of What You Want — You Might Get It*. Roanoke, VA: Stone Printing Co., 1970.

Seyle, H., *From Dream to Discovery*. New York: McGraw-Hill, 1964.

Stein, M., *Stimulating Creativity*. New York: Academic Press, 1974.

Toffler, A., *Future Shock*. New York: Random House, 1970.

Torrance, E., *Encouraging Creativity in the Classroom*. Dubuque, IA: W. C. Brown, 1970.

Westcott, M., *Toward a Contemporary Psychology of Intuition*. New York: Holt, Rinehart and Winston, 1968.

STUDY GUIDE

See page 6

See page 8

See page 24

See page 44

See page 44

Value   %

1. Supervisor training $\frac{1}{2}$ $\frac{1}{3}$ $\frac{1}{4}$ $\frac{1}{5}$ $\frac{1}{6}$ $\frac{1}{7}$ $\frac{1}{8}$ $\frac{1}{9}$ $\frac{1}{10}$ 1 = ___

2. Quality circles $\frac{2}{3}$ $\frac{2}{4}$ $\frac{2}{5}$ $\frac{2}{6}$ $\frac{2}{7}$ $\frac{2}{8}$ $\frac{2}{9}$ $\frac{2}{10}$ 2 = ___

3. Cross training $\frac{3}{4}$ $\frac{3}{5}$ $\frac{3}{6}$ $\frac{3}{7}$ $\frac{3}{8}$ $\frac{3}{9}$ $\frac{3}{10}$ 3 = ___

4. Piece work bonuses $\frac{4}{5}$ $\frac{4}{6}$ $\frac{4}{7}$ $\frac{4}{8}$ $\frac{4}{9}$ $\frac{4}{10}$ 4 = ___

5. Flex time $\frac{5}{6}$ $\frac{5}{7}$ $\frac{5}{8}$ $\frac{5}{9}$ $\frac{5}{10}$ 5 = ___

6. Four day week $\frac{6}{7}$ $\frac{6}{8}$ $\frac{6}{9}$ $\frac{6}{10}$ 6 = ___

7. New equipment $\frac{7}{8}$ $\frac{7}{9}$ $\frac{7}{10}$ 7 = ___

8. Air conditioning $\frac{8}{9}$ $\frac{8}{10}$ 8 = ___

9. Employee health spa $\frac{9}{10}$ 9 = ___

10. Child day care   10 = ___

See page 47

$$\frac{1}{2}\ \frac{1}{3}\ \frac{1}{4}\ \frac{1}{5}\ \frac{1}{6}\ \frac{1}{7}\ \frac{1}{8}\ \frac{1}{9}\ \frac{1}{10}\ \frac{1}{11}\ \frac{1}{12}\ \frac{1}{13}\ \frac{1}{14}\ \frac{1}{15}\ \frac{1}{16}\ \frac{1}{17}\ \frac{1}{18}$$

$$\frac{2}{3}\ \frac{2}{4}\ \frac{2}{5}\ \frac{2}{6}\ \frac{2}{7}\ \frac{2}{8}\ \frac{2}{9}\ \frac{2}{10}\ \frac{2}{11}\ \frac{2}{12}\ \frac{2}{13}\ \frac{2}{14}\ \frac{2}{15}\ \frac{2}{16}\ \frac{2}{17}\ \frac{2}{18}$$

$$\frac{3}{4}\ \frac{3}{5}\ \frac{3}{6}\ \frac{3}{7}\ \frac{3}{8}\ \frac{3}{9}\ \frac{3}{10}\ \frac{3}{11}\ \frac{3}{12}\ \frac{3}{13}\ \frac{3}{14}\ \frac{3}{15}\ \frac{3}{16}\ \frac{3}{17}\ \frac{3}{18}$$

$$\frac{4}{5}\ \frac{4}{6}\ \frac{4}{7}\ \frac{4}{8}\ \frac{4}{9}\ \frac{4}{10}\ \frac{4}{11}\ \frac{4}{12}\ \frac{4}{13}\ \frac{4}{14}\ \frac{4}{15}\ \frac{4}{16}\ \frac{4}{17}\ \frac{4}{18}$$

$$\frac{5}{6}\ \frac{5}{7}\ \frac{5}{8}\ \frac{5}{9}\ \frac{5}{10}\ \frac{5}{11}\ \frac{5}{12}\ \frac{5}{13}\ \frac{5}{14}\ \frac{5}{15}\ \frac{5}{16}\ \frac{5}{17}\ \frac{5}{18}$$

$$\frac{6}{7}\ \frac{6}{8}\ \frac{6}{9}\ \frac{6}{10}\ \frac{6}{11}\ \frac{6}{12}\ \frac{6}{13}\ \frac{6}{14}\ \frac{6}{15}\ \frac{6}{16}\ \frac{6}{17}\ \frac{6}{18}$$

$$\frac{7}{8}\ \frac{7}{9}\ \frac{7}{10}\ \frac{7}{11}\ \frac{7}{12}\ \frac{7}{13}\ \frac{7}{14}\ \frac{7}{15}\ \frac{7}{16}\ \frac{7}{17}\ \frac{7}{18}$$

$$\frac{8}{9}\ \frac{8}{10}\ \frac{8}{11}\ \frac{8}{12}\ \frac{8}{13}\ \frac{8}{14}\ \frac{8}{15}\ \frac{8}{16}\ \frac{8}{17}\ \frac{8}{18}$$

$$\frac{9}{10}\ \frac{9}{11}\ \frac{9}{12}\ \frac{9}{13}\ \frac{9}{14}\ \frac{9}{15}\ \frac{9}{16}\ \frac{9}{17}\ \frac{9}{18}$$

$$\frac{10}{11}\ \frac{10}{12}\ \frac{10}{13}\ \frac{10}{14}\ \frac{10}{15}\ \frac{10}{16}\ \frac{10}{17}\ \frac{10}{18}$$

$$\frac{11}{12}\ \frac{11}{13}\ \frac{11}{14}\ \frac{11}{15}\ \frac{11}{16}\ \frac{11}{17}\ \frac{11}{18}$$

$$\frac{12}{13}\ \frac{12}{14}\ \frac{12}{15}\ \frac{12}{16}\ \frac{12}{17}\ \frac{12}{18}$$

$$\frac{13}{14}\ \frac{13}{15}\ \frac{13}{16}\ \frac{13}{17}\ \frac{13}{18}$$

$$\frac{14}{15}\ \frac{14}{16}\ \frac{14}{17}\ \frac{14}{18}$$

$$\frac{15}{16}\ \frac{15}{17}\ \frac{15}{18}$$

$$\frac{16}{17}\ \frac{16}{18}$$

$$\frac{17}{18}$$

See page 49

Peas	Cauliflower	Dill	Carrots	Corn
Chives	Squash	Tomatoes	Parsley	Pumpkins
Rutabaga	Spinach	Radish	Zucchini	Lettuce
Potatoes	Collards	Cucumbers	Garlic	Gourds
Ground Cherries	Gladiolas	Pole Beans	Asparagus	Strawberries
Green Onions	Lima Beans	Rhubarb	Broccoli	_____
_____	_____	_____	_____	_____
_____	_____	_____	_____	_____

See page 50

1 Peas $\frac{1}{2}$ $\frac{1}{3}$ $\frac{1}{4}$ $\frac{1}{5}$ $\frac{1}{6}$ $\frac{1}{7}$ $\frac{1}{8}$ $\frac{1}{9}$ $\frac{1}{10}$ $\frac{1}{11}$ $\frac{1}{12}$

2 Parsley $\frac{2}{3}$ $\frac{2}{4}$ $\frac{2}{5}$ $\frac{2}{6}$ $\frac{2}{7}$ $\frac{2}{8}$ $\frac{2}{9}$ $\frac{2}{10}$ $\frac{2}{11}$ $\frac{2}{12}$

3 Cauliflower $\frac{3}{4}$ $\frac{3}{5}$ $\frac{3}{6}$ $\frac{3}{7}$ $\frac{3}{8}$ $\frac{3}{9}$ $\frac{3}{10}$ $\frac{3}{11}$ $\frac{3}{12}$

4 Cucumbers $\frac{4}{5}$ $\frac{4}{6}$ $\frac{4}{7}$ $\frac{4}{8}$ $\frac{4}{9}$ $\frac{4}{10}$ $\frac{4}{11}$ $\frac{4}{12}$

5 Dill $\frac{5}{6}$ $\frac{5}{7}$ $\frac{5}{8}$ $\frac{5}{9}$ $\frac{5}{10}$ $\frac{5}{11}$ $\frac{5}{12}$

6 Squash $\frac{6}{7}$ $\frac{6}{8}$ $\frac{6}{9}$ $\frac{6}{10}$ $\frac{6}{11}$ $\frac{6}{12}$

7 Lettuce $\frac{7}{8}$ $\frac{7}{9}$ $\frac{7}{10}$ $\frac{7}{11}$ $\frac{7}{12}$

8 Garlic $\frac{8}{9}$ $\frac{8}{10}$ $\frac{8}{11}$ $\frac{8}{12}$

9 Carrots $\frac{9}{10}$ $\frac{9}{11}$ $\frac{9}{12}$

10 Tomatoes $\frac{10}{11}$ $\frac{10}{12}$

11 Green Onions $\frac{11}{12}$

12 Broccoli

See page 55

| | VALUE | | | % | SATISFACTION | |
	MINE	YOURS		MINE	YOURS
1) Supervisor training	5			40	
2) Quality circles	5			50	
3) Cross training	7			30	
4) Piece work bonuses	4			55	
5) Flex time	7			35	
6) Four day week	4			30	
7) New equipment	1			50	
8) Air conditioning	7			20	
9) Employee health spa	0			0	
10) Child day care	5			65	

See page 58

1) Exercise program	How satisfied am I today with my exercise program?	30%	_____
2) Annual physicals	How satisfied am I with my health measurement program?	65%	_____
3) Employee assistance program	How satisfied am I with my company's EAP?	60%	_____
4) Health education program	How satisfied am I with my company's health education program?	50%	_____
5) Employee health spa	How satisfied am I with the availability of a spa?	50%	_____
6) Health goals	How satisfied am I with our goals program?	75%	_____
7) Stop smoking clinic	How satisfied am I with our stop smoking clinic?	0%	_____
8) Flex time	How satisfied am I with my present schedule?	80%	_____
9) Management commitment	How committed is upper management to improve health or how satisfied am I with their commitment?	85%	_____
10) Free meds	How satisfied am I with the cost of medication right now?	60%	_____
11) Exercise breaks	How satisfied am I with our scheduled exercise breaks?	25%	_____

12) Biofeedback	How satisfied am I with my knowledge of biofeedback and my access to it?	50% _____
13) Health pay	How satisfied am I with extra pay for staying healthy?	50% _____
14) Three week vacation	How satisfied am I with my present amount of paid vacation?	40% _____
15) Accumulate sick days	How satisfied am I with our unused sick pay accumulation policy?	100% _____
16) Relaxation breaks	How satisfied am I with opportunity to relax during my work day (coffee breaks)?	100% _____
17) Shorter hours	How satisfied am I with the length of my work day?	100% _____
18) Weight control clinic	How satisfied am I with my weight control program?	100% _____

See page 59

1) Peas	0	_____	7) Lettuce	10	_____
2) Parsley	30	_____	8) Garlic	100	_____
3) Cauliflower	75	_____	9) Carrots	80	_____
4) Cucumbers	50	_____	10) Tomatoes	20	_____
5) Dill	75	_____	11) Green Onions	60	_____
6) Squash	60	_____	12) Broccoli	60	_____

See page 63

```
                                  9
                                  8
                                  7
                                  6
  100  90  80  70  60             5   40  30  20  10  0
 _____
                                  4
                                  3
                                  2
                                  1
                                  0
```

See page 63

Ref #	Objective	Authors' Numbers		Readers' Numbers	
		Value	% S	Value	% S
1)	Supervisior training	5	40		
2)	Quality circles	5	50		
3)	Cross training	7	30		
4)	Piece work bonus	4	55		
5)	Flex time	7	35		
6)	Four day week	4	30		
7)	New equipment	1	50		
8)	Air conditioning	7	20		
9)	Employee health spa	0	0		
10)	Child day care	5	65		

See page 64

See page 67

See page 69

Ref #	Objective	Authors' Numbers		Readers' Numbers	
		Value	%	Value	%
1	Exercise programs	11	30		
2	Annual physicals	4	65		
3	Employee assistance	9	60		
4	Health education	14	50		
5	Employee health spa	9	50		
6	Health goals (MBO's)	14	75		
7	Stop smoking clinic	10	0		
8	Flexible time	10	80		
9	Management commitment	15	85		
10	Free medication	0	60		
11	Exercise breaks	9	25		
12	Biofeedback	4	50		
13	Health pay	2	50		
14	Three week vacation	15	40		
15	Accumulated sick pay	4	100		
16	Relaxation breaks	13	100		
17	Shorter hours	1	100		
18	Weight control clinic	9	80		

See page 70

See page 71

GIVENS (Upper Left)	OVERKILL (Lower Left)	GRIPES (Lower Right)	WANTS (Upper Right)

See page 72

		Authors' Numbers		Readers' Numbers	
Ref no.	Objective	Value	%	Value	%
1	Peas	9	0		
2	Parsley	6	30		
3	Cauliflower	2	75		
4	Cucumbers	8	50		
5	Dill	1	75		
6	Squash	7	60		
7	Lettuce	9	10		
8	Garlic	0	100		
9	Carrots	3	80		
10	Tomatoes	11	20		
11	Green Onions	6	40		
12	Broccoli	4	60		

See page 72

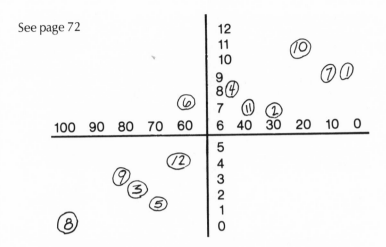

See page 82

Participant	A	B	C	D				Total	Avg.
1									
2									
3									
4									

See page 88

PRODUCTIVITY OBJECTIVES	AUTHORS #'s		GROUP #'s		YOUR NUMBERS	
Ref # OBJECTIVE	VALUE	%	VALUE	%	VALUE	%
1 Supervisor training	5	40	5.8	61	___	___
2 Quality circles	5	50	5.9	61	___	___
3 Cross training	7	30	6.6	29	___	___
4 Piece work bonus	4	55	5.2	67	___	___
5 Flex time	7	35	5.6	37	___	___
6 Four day week	4	30	5.5	29	___	___
7 New equipment	1	50	1.8	80	___	___
8 Air conditioning	7	20	3.4	30	___	___
9 SPA	0	0	1.7	25	___	___
10 Day care	5	65	3.3	75	___	___

See page 89

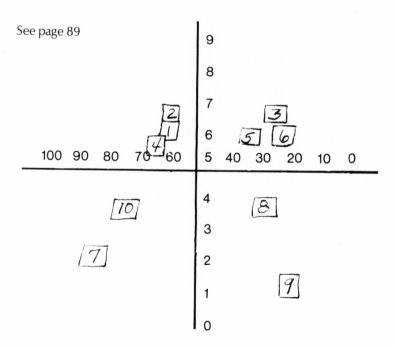

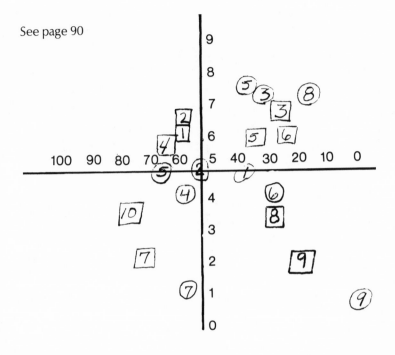

See page 90

See page 96

Potential Action	Cost	Benefit
	$, people, resources, etc.	$, PR, Morale, Productivity
1 Key Opportunity		
2 Alternate		
3 Alternate		
4 Alternate		
5 Alternate		

See page 97

Potential Objection	How to Overcome
1.	A B C
2.	A B C
3.	A B C

Notes

Notes